THE ROAD TO

The Road to Kill the Bill

Standing up for our rights to protest

Joseph Boyd

YOUCAXTON
PUBLICATIONS

ISBN 978-1-914424-11-3
Published by YouCaxton Publications 2021
YCBN: 01

YouCaxton Publications
www.youcaxton.co.uk

Picture Credits:
David Ellison (davidellisonphotography.com)
A Protest Walk | Battle of Barton Moss (thebattleofbartonmoss.com)

To all those who defend environmental degradation and human rights across the world

FOREWORD

JOE BOYD'S ACCOUNT of The Road to Kill the Bill goes to the heart of the current chapter in the long history of attacks on people protesting to protect their values, livelihoods and homes. Mainstream media has consistently underestimated the social and political importance of the anti-fracking campaigns which involve hundreds of local groups across the country. They do not understand how the determined, courageous and creative frontline activism of protestors, such as Joe, inspired local communities confronted with the threat of fracking to organise effective local action and protest. Current reports of various international climate conferences underlines the reality that we are all from round here – Planet Earth – but defence of it starts at each front door. Joe's remarkable journey from what was almost the dead end of addiction to successful litigation against INEOS and the richest man in the UK is a compelling human story, but he goes on to the heart of the dangers posed by global corporations and the emerging corporate state.

The history of spying, infiltration and provocation to weaken opposition to government goes back to Tudor times. The Road to Kill the Bill contains shocking insights into how the government, the police and industry use a variety of methods to divide and undermine the exercise of a democratic right to protest and oppose. The current 'spy cops' inquiry into the appalling behaviour of 139 undercover police officers since 1968 reminds us that this is still a key issue in any protest action.

We are in the second year of the chilling Johnson Government's experiment to see how far they can use the opportunity of Covid to test the passivity of British citizens, starting with the 'Stay at Home' message and ending with a Crime Bill which would effectively give the police unlimited powers to crush protest.

Joe's story hasn't ended. Although the threat of fracking may have gone, Joe wasn't surprised when we pointed to a report in Drill or Drop this month about shale gas companies working with universities to repurpose boreholes. This reinforces his view, shared with the late Ian R Crane, that the boreholes created as part of oil and gas exploration were a front for future deep geological disposal of toxic nuclear waste. The Infrastructure Act, combined with proposals in the Policing and Crime Bill, would further weaken any opposition to nuclear waste dumps.

Joe's combination of frontline involvement in a successful, locally-based campaign against fracking and his success against attempts to limit protest, combined with acute strategic analysis make The Road to Kill the Bill essential reading for anyone who is concerned about the state we are in.

Jon and Val Mager, Brighton, April 2021

Acknowledgments

I AM GRATEFUL to Diane Steels, Bob Dennett and Sue Marshall, for their support and first-hand experiences of incidents and observations provided for this book. Their testimonies substantiate their journey and mine, for those who will attempt to continue their gaslighting, with fantasist labels, even now long after our Court of Appeal success. Their bravery for assisting in these works shows great courage, considering all they've endured.

Thank you to all my legal team, for having the faith to work with me, in our long but successful fight for justice. Rosa Curling, Anna Dews, Heather Williams, Blinne Ní Ghrálaigh and Jennifer Robinson and their legal offices at Leigh Day, Matrix and Doughty Street Chambers. I'm grateful to all the people who helped fund our legal challenge, wherever in the world you reside.

I want to thank Jon and Val Mager for their bare witnessing to events at the High Court, their personal contributions and support for many years, and for proof-reading and writing the foreward for this book. Thanks to Benjamin Dean and Sharon Whale for their work on injunctions, and the solidarity and friendship they've showed throughout. When many people had succumbed to the manipulation and only a few remained, they stood up and were counted.

I'm grateful to my family for their unwavering support throughout, backing me to see justice through, in many ways. My gratitude goes to Victoria Aeyn and Wayne Paolucci, for standing up at times when we faced an onslaught of abuse for defending our rights to protest.

Another person deserving of a mention is Helen Chuntso who set the foundations for our legal team challenge to INEOS; without her the challenge may have never occurred. There are far too many people around the country to thank personally, who played their part in my journey, but I'm privileged to know each and every one of them. Thank you to Ella Knight and Bob Fowke at You Caxton publications for their committed time and effort to finalise these works.

Finally, I'm indebted to the fine skills of Emily Anderson, who worked closely with me on the final edit, for many hours, against the clock.

Contents

INTRODUCTION

AFTER MIRACULOUSLY SURVIVING my tumultuous life of serious mental health issues and addictions, a working-class lad growing up in one of the roughest areas of Liverpool, I was given a second chance to make something of myself. In 2012, I set about beginning a new life of recovery, opportunity and optimism for the future. I began an Open University degree in Environmental Studies in 2013 and found out about the controversial onshore oil and gas extraction method called fracking. By then, large parts of the US and Australia had been decimated by this destructive and dangerous method, which fractures rock underground at high pressure to extract the oil or gas, causing earthquakes and polluting farmland, water and air for miles around. Suddenly, it was coming to a site just over thirty miles from my home.

Strongly compelled to stop this toxic industry from getting a foothold in this country, my inspiration for telling my story started in 2013, when I became a frontline activist at the Barton Moss drilling site, to the west of Manchester. I lived on protection camps outside drilling sites twenty-four hours a day, in all weathers, there for whatever protest was deemed necessary and as an information point for local communities across Northern England. I and many others involved in the fight against fracking regularly slow-walked lorries in and out of drilling sites, and did hours-long lock-ons, to slow the industry down. I also spoke at many local meetings to inform communities about what was happening in their area and galvanise support for the protests.

When I wasn't on the frontline, but at home working on my studies, I was campaigning online, raising awareness through social media and watching the many livestreams of the demonstrations at various sites including Upton, Crawberry Hill and Kirby Misperton in Yorkshire, Preston New Road, near Blackpool, in Lancashire, as well as other sites in the south of England.

I met a lot of knowledgeable, dedicated and supportive people along the way, but it wasn't all fun and games, by any means. I experienced violent clashes with the police, who arrested and physically assaulted me many times, and I was targeted by others in the anti-fracking movement. At a point when local resistance was really affecting the industry, certain key players were sabotaging our progress in a subtle but significant way. Suspicions arose about police and security services infiltration, corporate manipulation and agent provocateurs embedded within the movement to paint a negative picture of protestors in the media. The people I have mentioned in this book are a small selection compared to those I have omitted who were also complicit in the attempt to deter any activist resistance to unethical businesses.

As divisions between campaigners increased, many activists around the country, including myself, experienced gaslighting and smear campaigns that people are still recovering from to this day. However, my flexible timetable due to my ongoing university studies, enabled me to become an expert in monitoring these discursive actions of campaigners on a day-by-day basis, both in person and online, giving me a real insight into key people, allegiances and responses.

Nowhere was this discursive operation more prevalent than in Lancashire, from 2014 onwards. When large Non-Governmental Organisations (NGOs) such as Reclaim the Power joined in the fight, it might have looked like more power to the people. But after many big direct actions involving these groups, court injunctions to limit protest were served soon after, whereby anyone who disrupted the activities of a drilling company could face a large fine or prison sentence. My research into these NGOs, who I initially thought was there to do good, shocked me.

What started as a desire to stop fracking in my local area, ended up in a legal battle to protect our human rights. Between 2014 and 2019, I attended the High Court of England and Wales on seven occasions and once at the Royal Courts of Justice Appeal Courts, regarding injunctions stopping our right to protest. I'm the only person in the UK to be at all these hearings. Two hearings came early in my campaign in 2014, where I was simply an onlooker because of my campaigning inexperience. In the subsequent three High Court appearances, I was directly involved with preparing a defence case with a dedicated team of environmentalists without legal representation. In the final two High Court appearances and the Appeal Court, I was the challenger, represented by the country's best human rights, public and international law lawyers, defending Articles 10 and 11 of the Human Rights Act.

These freedoms of expression, assembly and association, have continued to be eroded ever since. The emergence of the climate change protest group Extinction Rebellion in 2018 has given the government all the evidence of disruption and chaos it needs to bring in further severe restrictions to protest, with its Police, Crime, Sentencing and Courts Bill, which many people are protesting about in a bid to Kill the Bill. However, the even more chilling Covert Human Intelligence Sources Act Act 2021, has recently been passed by Parliament, which has raised alarm bells for many that we are being taken into an authoritarian state.

I was motivated to write about what I have experienced because it's a substantial and valuable piece of research and on-the-ground evidence that few others could provide in such detail. I almost dropped the idea of writing about it in 2019 but my subconscious kept nudging away at me until at the end of 2020, when it all had to come out. This story belongs to everyone anyway.

My aim is to emphasise the importance of personal sovereignty in the challenges that lie ahead. In these strange, chaotic times, I want to show that local, grassroots resistance and personal sovereignty can and must create change; to reveal proof that not everyone is who they say they are; and to warn that our human rights are blatantly being eroded and have been for many years, step by step by change agents. From a historical sense, this book only covers my first-hand experience for just under a decade, ending in Spring 2021. Many people will have had similar experiences but been unable to speak out, for fear of gaslighting, in many social justice movements over this time too.

Just as I have throughout this story, we all need to keep questioning what we are presented with by the mainstream media, big businesses and governments. We are in a precarious position in England, right now, and I hope my story of one man taking on the state, highlighting the corruption in even the supposedly most well-meaning of movements, wakes people up in time to stop the slide into Stasi Britain.

Some people reading this might think, "Why have I not heard about any of this?" That is the real purpose of my story. Censorship on social media is rife, mainstream media are complicit, change agents manipulate and NGOs are almost dormant. Therefore, the only way I could tell my story, so that people would see the orchestrated attack on our rights to protest, was through writing a book. I decided to self-publish rather than risk the possibility of publisher censorship. Creeping authoritarianism, in my experience, leaves minimal options for non-fictional research and compelling evidence such as this. I hope this book inspires others to come forward and help humanity at this crucial time and be an incentive for other writers to tell us their stories.

One

A Life of Addiction Before Activism

FOR TWENTY YEARS my life had been hell, and I wanted to play no further part in it. I could have turned around, there and then, and died soon after, but something happened which made me believe my time here was for a reason. Despite losing my Catholic school teachings long before, I was now certain that I had been saved from death by a spiritual force, for some other purpose. What that purpose was I had no idea, but I did know something in my life had to change.

From the ages of eleven to thirty-nine, my life was mainly about gambling, alcohol and drugs. I started gambling at secondary school, playing pitch'n'toss in the playground at break time, before moving on to horse racing. Just a pre-teen, I gambled every morning and afternoon, standing outside the betting shop to get customers to put bets on for me. I enjoyed the thrill of the buzz from winning and believed it was the path to my riches. I started drinking at fourteen, generally just sitting on a field with friends, then moved on aged fifteen, to smoking cannabis every day. Consequently, my path was chaotic and unstable. I reeled from one drama to another crisis, hurting people along the way, losing most of my belongings, gambling away anything I earned. I was a thief, too. I would shoplift most days on the way home from school, at the shopping centre in Wallasey, half way between school and home.

I went to prison three times, in my early twenties. On the first occasion, just twenty years old, I told the courts to send me to jail, as I had no intention of paying the fine or doing sixty hours community service for burglary of a shop. So that's where they sent me, for sixty days. I needed it. Many thought I was crazy for wanting to go to prison, and my thinking was often insane at this point. I viewed prison as an escape from my daily obsession with my destructive addictions. However, I quickly realised jail wouldn't change anything, when I still managed to place a bet from inside. No matter what I did or where I tried to hide, I could not escape it. I always had a plan with gambling, dreaming that this time would be different. But as soon as I placed a bet, I lost all control. When the bell rang for the greyhound race, or a commentator said the horses were going in the stalls, I would be off, like a lunatic, with all sensible strategy out the window.

Winning a load of money made me feel like a rock star, splashing the cash, but it would only last that night. The next day I would go back and lose everything I had won and more, and that jubilation, invincibility, and elation would be gone, shame and misery creeping into its place. Every time, I would tell myself that was it, game over, I would not bet again. But I always did.

Despite this stupidity, I would say my intelligence was high in all other areas. I had many jobs, starting as an electrical apprentice when I was fifteen. I was one of only forty people to get that apprenticeship, from 750 applications. But I was unable to stay the course and quit after fifteen months: the pattern of my career path was set. In different positions, I earned good money, but I was always penniless soon after being paid. I simply couldn't sustain or complete any achievements from start to finish.

After years of turmoil in my inner and outer worlds, the two weeks preceding my awakening to my new life was intensely chaotic. I was drinking eight to ten cans of strong a lager a day whilst convincing myself I was happy and content. But I wasn't happy at all. I was at rock bottom. The problem with gambling is the invisible nature of the illness. Drug addiction and alcoholism are more obvious to see. But, unless you've been or known a compulsive gambler, the signs and struggles are less easy to spot. I may have looked like I was having a great time, but my mental health was on the floor. I was using booze to escape life: in reality I was miserable.

One evening, sick of all the shame, the lies and emotional pain, I searched for a rope to hang myself but could not even manage to find a rope to do that, so I hoped some garment material would suffice, which it did not. Another evening, drunk out of my mind, I took myself to a hospital A&E department asking them for help because my mind was yet again thinking thoughts of suicide. They said I was agitated, something I loudly contested at the time, so they had me arrested. The next day, during my release from the police station, the sergeant suggested I go back to the hospital and ask for help again, now that I was sober. I went home, got changed, and headed to the hospital, where I met with a mental health crisis team. They told me I was okay and that I just had a housing problem and sent me home. Bewildered at their lack of care, and feeling like I had no other options left, I walked the seven miles home, then went straight for a drinking session.

Bizarrely, the final day of what I now see as the old life was probably the happiest day I had ever had. I felt all the worries of the world had dropped from my shoulders as I drank a few beers in the sun, sitting in the backyard of a house full of drugs and alcohol, in one of the most deprived boroughs in the country. But later that night, the darkness of my emotions took over, the pain and turmoil I was going through, the futility of my life, tipped me over the edge. Aged thirty nine, I decided to end it all. Rummaging through the bathroom cabinet and kitchen draws at the house, I found all the paracetamol and co-codamol that I could find, and took them all. I have no idea how many I took, but I slumped down on a chair and slipped into an unconscious state.

I woke up the following day on a hospital ward. Somebody had called an ambulance and I'd been saved. The next day, I was offered a fourteen day stay in a treatment centre. These places are usually only for drug and alcohol rehab, rather than for gambling, but now that I was drinking eight or more strong lagers a day, I fitted the category. The first few days were a welcome break from my normal day-to-day

3

activities, and I used the time to reflect remorsefully on how I must have made my family feel.

After several days, the fog was beginning to clear in my mind. I was starting to wonder if the universe might have other plans for me because I was still alive. Why was I spared death? What was coming next? However, the fog was still not clear enough for me to completely engage with everything. On the fourth evening, I had the option of listening to someone from Narcotics Anonymous (NA), but I refused as I did not believe I had a narcotic problem even though I took cocaine and other party drugs from time to time. I had heard of Gamblers Anonymous (GA) before though; people had long told me I needed to attend. I was never convinced, I just thought I was an unlucky gambler.

Two nights later, a lad aged about forty came in from Cocaine Anonymous (CA), and this time for whatever reason, I chose to attend and listen to what he had to say. It was a decision that changed my life. I completely resonated with everything he said. It was as if this speaker was talking about me. I knew then that there was hope, there was a solution to my suffering that had helped many others just like me: recovery. It was a light bulb moment in over two decades of darkness. The speaker left me a small Alcoholics Anonymous book and told me to read it and judge for myself if I fitted the description of someone with an alcoholic's mind. When I changed the word 'alcohol' for 'gambling', I could not deny it, everything undoubtedly described me. I knew that I had to attend Anonymous meetings; otherwise, I would quickly be back to where I had been just a few days earlier.

Grateful to all the staff who supported me, I left the detox centre after a fortnight and was allocated a housing space for drug and alcohol addicts, to continue the next steps of my recovery. Staff strictly told me that with just one relapse, I would be out. I honoured this approach because I lived with four others in similar positions and knew a personal deterioration could jeopardise everyone else. I had weekly update meetings with my designated support worker Annie, so she was able to support me when required. My primary obsession was gambling though, so I knew I could manage no drinking, yet I still respectfully followed all the rules and never touched a drop.

On my departure from the treatment centre, I also received a phone number for a day centre for one-to-one counselling and group work, if I was interested, which I was. It was a time in my life full of opportunities - and I grasped them with both hands. At the sessions, the supervisor was a lovely ex-alcoholic named Colette, who had previously lived a tumultuous life, just as I had, with alcohol rather than gambling. She told me later, when I entered the room for the first time, she thought, 'Oh no'. I may have not had a bet or a drink for just over two weeks, but the pain and misery of the last twenty years were still raw and apparently evident in my demeanor.

That Thursday, I went to the CA meeting; I had promised myself I would go, although still full of fear. I hardly said a word but knew I had to listen, and returned the following week. For the next ninety days, I attended over one hundred meetings, sometimes two a day within the recovery fellowships, ranging from GA, NA, CA and Alcoholics Anonymous (AA), all whilst also going to the day centre five days a week. My tenacity surprised me, but as my confidence grew, I embraced life for the first time in many years. Discovering that I could release deep feelings and long-buried emotions slowly for the world to see, and not be rejected, but be understood, made it easier to be my true authentic self. I was determined to go down this healing journey to uncover my truth. So, life now was all about recovery. I hoped that the more sessions I attended, the less chance I had of going backwards. After four months of dedicated work on myself, I graduated from the day centre. I had built the cornerstone to a new life, yet there was still much work to do.

In February 2013, while still living in supported housing, I began a degree with the Open University in Environmental Studies, which, near the end, changed to International Studies. I had always wanted to study for a degree and this helped keep me focused on working towards a goal.

By now, I had attended about two-hundred various Anonymous meetings, so I felt strong enough to scale down to one or two per week. By April, I was able to leave the supported housing, so I said my goodbyes and thanked the Phoenix Futures staff for all their support and faith in me. No way could I have done it without them. Whether recovery comes down to the individual or not, I needed that solid foundation that only support from professionals and recovering addicts can provide.

Now, for the first time in about ten years, I could live independently and continue studying whilst building a new life. I was hoping I would be able to have a nice home, with a career, which enabled me to travel, and have a better relationship with friends and family. Where my life took me from this point was not how I envisaged at all.

Two

How I Became Involved in the Anti-Fracking Campaign

I FIRST LEARNED of the technology known as hydraulic fracturing, in my first year of undergraduate study, whilst researching environmental issues. Informally, referred to as 'fracking', it is an unconventional well stimulation technique that fractures the bedrock below the surface to release gas. The term 'unconventional' refers to horizontal drilling prior to fracturing the shale rock with small explosions then forcing fluid and sand into the rock to fracture it and release oil or gas, in contrast to conventional vertical well extraction. I found out from research that there were dangers to the environment - to water, air and land - from the method which had already run rampant in parts of America and Australia.

Proponents of the industry - mostly oil and gas companies and the government - said it was a well regulated industry with nothing to worry about regarding local environments, plus we needed the gas for energy security reasons. The government would always cite Royal Society reports, which said the industry would be safe if done correctly. On further research, I had found this was not the case, and the risk to the environment too great for something which we did not need at all. I felt strongly compelled that I should oppose it.

My intention was to participate in as many areas of the anti-fracking campaign as possible. I had not campaigned about anything before but I wanted a true reflection of what was really happening on the ground, not from the mainstream media or vested interests, which I could straight away see were biased.

I first came across a protest against fracking on social media, in the late summer of 2013. This protest was taking place in a leafy village called Balcombe in West Sussex against Cuadrilla Resources. One opinion poll showed that around eighty two percent of the village residents who responded, were against fracking, yet Cuadrilla was just about to drill on the peripherals of this beautiful village. There were two protest camps at Balcombe, one at the side of the road near the drilling and site and one a short walk away, set up in an occupied field by Reclaim the Power (RTP).

My earliest recollection of those daily protests was the arrest of the Green Party MP for Brighton Pavillion, Caroline Lucas. Watching her get picked up off the tarmac and taken away by police on television, I was inspired because she was standing up for her beliefs. I don't think I'd ever seen politicians do that before, certainly not on the mainstream news.

Day after day, campaigners would slow-walk lorries to and from the site to delay Cuadrilla's operations. However inconvenient it might have been to some, this successful technique was a legitimate form of protest. My initial feeling was that short term disruption such as this, far outweighed the long-term environmental degradation caused by this toxic industry. I did not think for one minute that this protest technique of slow-walking would eventually become the single most contentious issue for me and many others in the years ahead.

The main Balcombe protests started in July and ended in September, with 126 arrests of campaigners in just sixty two days. Under Section 14 (S14) of the Public Order Act, the police had the power to arrest campaigners if they ignored restrictions imposed on the protest. S14 imposes conditions on public assemblies on how long and where you can protest. According to the Act, these restrictions are, "to prevent serious public disorder, serious criminal damage or serious disruption to the life of the community".

According to lawyers who were representing arrestees, these events were a turning point in policing of protests because it was the first time S14 was used to mass arrest during a protest; in doing so it had criminalised protest. This section of the Public Order Act 1986 being used resulted in peaceful campaigners being arrested and dragged through the court system for months before many were acquitted. From what I could observe from home, the vast majority of the campaigners detained were white and middle class, not the usual demographic to be dragged to jail.

I lived too far away from Balcombe to support these protests in person. Plus, I was still studying. But I tried to contribute online as much as possible, sharing livestreams and articles to raise awareness. I would've loved to have gone to the solidarity day there, organised by Frack Off, as coachloads of people were going from different parts of the country, yet I couldn't find one from Liverpool. So, it wasn't to be. But I was deeply drawn to the campaign and wanted to help further. I promised myself that if the industry ever headed to Northern England, I would get involved in some pro-active way. Meanwhile I researched more about it and continued with my studies.

Fracking in the UK first gained wider attention in Spring 2011, when two earthquake tremors were felt across Lancashire. The area surrounding onshore oil and gas drilling company Cuadrilla's operations at the Preese Hall well near Blackpool, experienced two quakes reaching magnitudes of 1.5 and 2.3 on the Richter scale. This raised the alarm of many people who had not campaigned before, among them a man called Geza Tarjani, who later changed his name to Geza Frackman, and Bob Dennett who went on to be founder of Frack Free Lancashire (FFL). On Facebook anti-fracking pages, Geza reported damage to his house from the operations and set out to be at the forefront of challenging the industry. The quakes were felt up to ten miles away, but especially at a school just 1,500ft away and at Weeton Army barracks, the closest homes to the well. During Cuadrilla's early involvement in these fracking operations in Lancashire, some 884,000 gallons of toxic waste were dumped in the Manchester Ship Canal, before the Environment Agency finally stopped them. How many people's houses were damaged from the quakes is hard to know because the industry had a history globally of getting people to sign non-disclosure agreements in return for compensation claims.

Seeing pictures of thousands of wells across the landscape of parts of America and Australia was enough shocking evidence for me of what would happen to the countryside in the UK if we allowed the industry to take hold. I believed no amount of regulation could make this industry safe never mind self-regulation, and I intended to get involved in the fight against it.

In November 2013, while watching the local BBC North West Tonight (NWT) evening news, I saw a news item about a couple of campaigners, who I later came to know as Mark and Shaun. They set up a protest camp, similar to what I had seen at Balcombe, against fracking company IGas, who were about to exploratory drill in Salford, near Manchester. These lads were clearing shrub at the side of a public footpath, in miserable conditions and soaking wet clothes. Winter in Salford is considerably bleaker than the sunny carnival in Sussex seen a few months before. My first thoughts were that people won't sleep in tents at the side of the road in winter. It would be hard to motivate anyone to join the protest camp, surely.

On local TV, Mark was asking local people to get involved with the campaign. I had just finished my first year of study a few weeks earlier, so nothing was holding me back until my next module began in February 2014. The timing and location were perfect for me, this site was just over thirty miles from my home. I spent the weekend preparing myself to visit the camp, now being called the Barton Moss Protection Camp. For how long I'd go, I had no idea. With zero camping equipment, I borrowed a tent, which I was later to realise was useless. I packed a rucksack with warm and waterproof clothes and psyched myself up for an adventure. On reflection, I had not really evaluated the risks to my recovery, I just felt compelled to go. I had been training to run a marathon for the previous three months, so I was in good shape physically and mentally. I was on a strict endurance plan, with a strict diet to accompany it, so felt strong.

I was heading to the Greater Manchester backyard of Salford, pretty brave for a Scouser, given the rivalry between the two football clubs. But fear could play no part as I had already decided in my first year of study, that future generations will judge me on how radical I was in my efforts to protect the environment during my brief stay on this earth. Furthermore, I was more than aware that when democracy fails, protesting is the only avenue left open for us all.

The one and only time I had camped out before was over twenty years earlier. On that occasion, three friends and I, all in our late teens, set off from Wallasey on bicycles, for the weekend to a town called Ruthin, in North Wales. But with heavy rain soaking us through and darkness descending, we stopped in Loggerheads a few miles away from our final destination to set shelter for the night. In a rush to get out of the rain, we stupidly decided to leave the tent's outer sheet off and take cover just with the inner. In the dark we had also pitched on a steepish hill, so the next morning, we awoke completely drenched and with a swimming pool at the bottom of the tent. That morning we packed up and cycled on to Ruthin, found a launderette to dry everything, and then decided to cycle the fifty-mile journey straight back home. So put off by our one night's camping fiasco, we rode all the way back home that same day along the busy A55, which looking back was insane in itself.

The whole experience put me off camping so much, I never even attended a music festival or camped out again. Yet, here I was two decades later in winter planning to sleep on the side of a road in Salford to protest against the oil and gas industry for an unspecific amount of time, in a tent. Recovery or not, I was clearly still insane.

Three

Arriving at Barton Moss Protection Camp

ON MONDAY THE twenty-fifth of November 2013, I headed for Liverpool Lime Street train station to catch a train to Irlam with total apprehension. Irlam was the nearest train station to the Barton Moss Protection Camp, in the semi-rural, working-class community of Irlam and Cadishead. From Irlam, still over four miles away from the site, I boarded a bus with my rucksack, tent and bedding for the fifteen minute journey to the top of Barton Moss Road on the A57. As I was leaving the bus, a middle-aged lady got off at the same time. We smiled at each other.

"Where are you headed?" she asked in a Mancunian accent.

"Barton Moss anti-fracking camp," I said.

"Me too," she replied. "I'm Brigitte. I've been supporting Frack Free Greater Manchester for a while."

In the ten minute walk to the camp, on the tarmac I would tread every inch of in the coming months, she told me this was her first visit to camp, but she had been following the national campaign for some time. This warm and welcoming meeting was the confirmation I needed that I was in precisely the right place at the right time. Even the miserable, cold weather couldn't put a dampener on my buoyant spirit.

The protest camp was located on the edge of a public footpath, just over halfway between the busy A57 and the IGas drilling site, which ran adjacent to the M62 between Liverpool and Manchester. Tents, tables and chairs had been set up along the verge, some four-hundred yards from the M62 itself and alongside which all trucks had to pass to enter the site

The locals know this place as the Salford Mosses and have for centuries walked and enjoyed these lands for many hobbies and traditions. This land has the largest Grade one and two farmlands in England and the most extensive woodland in Greater Manchester. Furthermore, it's of significant wildlife interest of farmland birds and remnants in a nationally declining lowland peat bog habitat. As I took in my rural surroundings, I was shocked to think this area was about to be ruined by fracking.

Mark and Shaun, who I had seen on TV, were there to greet me that first afternoon, along with another guy called Gary, who had the comfort of his own camper van. A local Salfordian named Bob visited us for support, bringing supplies including food and a bag of socks and we all chatted for a couple of hours. Everyone seemed so welcoming including the local community.

I picked a spot and set up my useless single skin tent which wasn't long enough for my six-foot, three-inch frame. There was no kitchen built on camp at this point, so locals dropped off some bags of chips, fish and pies from the chippy, so we had warm food in us. Gary offered me a drink of ginger wine to keep warm in his van before settling down in my tent. I had not drunk in over a year, so limited myself to a couple of glasses. I tossed and turned on an uneven hard floor, with droplets of rain slowly seeping through my tent. *What was I doing here? I hate camping. What use can I be here? What's going to happen?* Doubts and fears ran through my mind as I remembered my comfy, warm bed at home.

The next morning I arose from my tent about seven o' clock to see a campfire burning and a kettle on the stove and people gathering for the day ahead. Other people who I had not met the day before had joined us, as word had spread that trucks would be heading to the drilling site that morning with their first deliveries. One of the tents next to me on the grass verge, was Ian R Crane's, who I had watched broadcast a lot from Balcombe. An ex-oil and gas executive, he was widely seen by many as highly knowledgeable about the fracking industry. Now, here he was camping near me and reporting events directly from the protest. Ian was not on camp this first day of protest, as he would always be in Plymouth for his weekly Fracking Nightmare show one day a week broadcasted on UK Column. Over the next few weeks and months, our friendship would grow deeper, a great mutual respect and trust developed between us, and over the following days and weeks you could set a clock by our appearance at the top of the road waiting for protest to begin with camp member Diane Steels.

The campaign's collective aim was to slow down the industry as long as possible to give us enough time to be able to educate the general public of the industry's risk and harms to the local environment. The mainstream media usually gave a biased view favouring the industry, and the Conservative government were all out for shale gas, following its neoliberal counterparts in the US and Australia, where the industry had already decimated swathes of the landscape. I suggested anyone do thirty minutes of meaningful research into the subject, and if they cared for the environment they would come to the same conclusion I had - and hopefully want to join us in stopping shale in its tracks.

The plan on my first day was to do some slow-walking, a technique of protest deemed lawful and used to great effect at Balcombe that summer. So I drank my mandatory morning brew and headed up Barton Moss Road just after nine o' clock to the junction of the A57 to gather with some forty or fifty others to wait for the lorries.

Just after eleven o' clock that morning, a convoy of trucks with site equipment began to arrive, flanked by Greater Manchester Police (GMP) Tactical Aid Unit (TAU). The everyday police officers were not alone; there were also police liaison officers (in blue bibs). They are a self-proclaimed liaison group between themselves and the campaigners. I soon realised they were there to try and soften us up on behalf of commanding officers to hinder our aims by gathering intelligence on campaigners, and control the protest.

There were also Forward Intelligence Teams (FIT) there to collect visual evidence of the protest, as long as it didn't discriminate against the coppers, of course. Many campaigners had videoing equipment pointed on the police as well, to evidence any of their wrongdoings. Finally, we had the presence of the various commanding officers, Gold, Silver or Bronze. The Commanding Officer in attendance was generally a Bronze Commander; Gold and Silver would typically be sat in some office back at police headquarters. I am not sure who the commanding officer was on day one, but most days after that, it was Bronze.

The Silver Commander at the time was Mark Roberts, Chief Superintendent of GMP. Roberts had begun his police career at GMP in 1993. During Robert's twenty-year career there, he had led a syndicate on the Force Major Investigation Team (FMIT) as Head of Investigations at the North West Counter Terrorism Unit. He was also a public order and firearms strategic commander and in charge of the tactical response to the 2011 riots in Manchester and Salford, where he was also Silver Commander. No denying, Roberts was experienced in protests and would play a leading role in the police's strategic operations at Barton Moss. I would later realise his part in anti-fracking demonstrations and other issues did not end there.

After half an hour of non-negotiation and the Commanding Officer telling us to step aside for the lorries, you could feel the tension in the air as over a hundred police officers disembarked their TAU vans. As the police formed a line across the footpath, my first ever slow-walk was about to begin. We began to move slowly down the pathway, singing and playing musical instruments. The atmosphere was eerie; I didn't know what might happen next. Resolutely, we continued slowly down the footpath, passing the camp and along to the drilling site.

The walk took just under two-hours, before the lorries entered the drilling site and two hours out, with an hour break in between, whilst the lorries unloaded. That first slow-walk, I kept my distance from the front line, some five to ten metres away, observing, whilst building up courage and learning my fellow campaigners' techniques. I had not been in a situation with this amount of police before, but I didn't trust them and was very wary of their actions, having experienced what they can do to you in the back of a van and a police station, years earlier. Furthermore, I was only used to police officers having the upper hand in all situations. But would this be the case today?

There were four arrests made on that first day, one quite brutally, on the walk to the drilling site just forty yards from the entrance, when a young lad Robbie was pushed to the ground by a group of officers. After witnessing the marks all over this arrestee's face and the arrest of others, I knew I would have to stay longer for support.

We did this protest almost every weekday, morning and afternoon. The Commanding Officer would order us to keep moving, and we would respond with, "everyone's moving". The phrase 'keep moving' would later be the title of a damming report by the University of York and Liverpool John Moores University into the policing of the protests, some time after the Barton Moss protest had ended in February 2016.

Most Wednesdays, Saturdays and Sundays were days off from protest unless the police tried to catch camp members off guard by aiding the movement of a vital piece of drilling equipment into the site. I quickly established myself on camp as the person who would wake everyone up each morning, at seven o' clock in almost military fashion, banging on caravan windows and shouting outside peoples tents. The kettle was always on for them, though. If the local community was funding us to be there, I felt it was only right to be up and ready before the lorries arrived so we could slow-walk every one. Not all camp members appreciated the rude awakenings, especially if they had a hangover, but it never stopped me; after all, the spirits of the land were protecting me, it seemed.

I used my building experience to build the kitchen area and shelters with camp members and Bob, who I had met on the first night. We used various bits of wood, pallets and tarpaulin donated by kind locals to make shelving for food donations and somewhere to cook and make teas on.

My first brew of the day was usually in the company of a man named George Brown, who went by the name of 'Silver Fox' or as most called him, Foxy. Brown was always moaning, but I just thought that was old age, as he was of the retirement age. He claimed he had been an environmentalist for many years after leaving the special forces and his wife bankrupting him. The majority of camp members had met him previously at Balcombe, where he was also a resident. We got on great when he was there, but he would often go off camp, leaving me to look after his tent, which was much bigger than mine, so I didn't mind. Tammy Samede was also a regular on camp and was close friends with Brown. A guy called Yellow Belly and another called Kieran Dunne, also showed up and were frequent camp members. Another person who joined camp went by the name of Kate McCann (Fargo, Brian Pegg), who turned up in a Sky broadband van, claiming he was giving up work and joining us. His work van was picked up some days later by a recovery vehicle. At times, there was around thirty people living on camp.

Four

The Beginning of the National Activists Discourse

THROUGHOUT DECEMBER, FIVE arrests were made a day, on average. Most days you could hear the Bronze Commander ordering his Inspector to do 'one more' or 'two more' arrests. These arrests invariably targeted individuals outside the North West region, who could be portrayed discursively as outsiders to those watching the regional BBC News. I firmly believed at the time this was why the police never targeted me, so local people avoided the arrest statistics. Years later, I would be proved right.

That there were arrests at all genuinely alarmed me; after all the environment belongs to everyone and has no borders. Surely anyone from anywhere was allowed to protect it. What does it matter if you live one-hundred miles away? Even though I was from the North West, my home was thirty miles from the drill site itself; was I deemed local enough to come here and protect this region?

I was starting to see how local communities could easily be manipulated by a big business if they could not call on others' support and expertise. How easy could it be for an oil and gas industry representative to deceive the community and lead them to believe they had everything under control? Before long, that community finds out that they were actively facilitating the industry and authorities in the destruction of the environment. 'Outsiders' who may already know more about the issue are essential in the fight. Moreover, do we not have the right to protect the environment when we visit a National Park in another county or even abroad? Despite not being arrested at the site, I arrived home after a Christmas and New Year away at camp to find a card with a Merseyside Police phone number to contact dropped through my letterbox. I phoned them straight away, but both intelligence officers who wanted to get in touch were on holiday. A couple of weeks later, they caught up with me on my next thirty-six-hour break from camp at my home. I told them that I would continue to resist the industry in no uncertain terms, and I would only stop when the fracking industry had. I'd heard that police knocking on campaigners' doors was not unusual; I saw it as an intimidation tactic and a wasted journey on their behalf. But did it mean my actions were having an impact? Other protestors were also targeted at their home addresses. It seemed that the police had become private security for the fracking industry.

Every four weeks at Barton Moss, I saw the police operational tactics change. The first month, we knew the policing of our protest would be fairly consistent each day. Then, one day when I was at home, I saw online that the slow-walk was fast and dangerous, with campaigners out of breath at the end of the demonstration. GMP also installed a female inspector to direct the TAU, which made the officers more senseless, as if they were out to impress their female superior with the minimum of five-arrests-a-day.

Then, on the fourth of January 2014 the police claimed campaigners fired a flare from the camp at a police helicopter approaching Barton Aerodrome, which ran adjacent to our residence. This alleged flare incident was denied by camp, at a time when I had gone home. If someone had fired a flare at a police helicopter with five police officers on board, the camp would have been swarming with cops within minutes, surely? No one on camp would be able to deny it, because a flare can be seen from miles away and stays in the air long enough to take a picture of. There were usually somewhere between sixty and eighty GMP officers at the protest most days, so I'm sure it would not have taken much of a decision to send a couple of vans of coppers to the camp to investigate straight away.

However, the police took no action for two-days, not even attending the camp on the night in question. Instead, Mark Roberts the Chief Superintendent (Silver Commander) of GMP, created a public and media discourse, which we ended up calling 'flaregate'. Camp members and national campaigners both saw this as a new tactic of the police to allow them to raid the camp, hoping they could find ways to discredit us further through the media.

At the time, some campaigners who had a historical knowledge of environmental protests were theorising that the false flare accusation could be the direct work of Amanda Webster. Webster had national expertise in advising the police and government on various protest groups, in particular those of us against controversial building and development projects, including the Manchester Airport extension. She was known in social and environmental justice activism circles as the 'protest buster' for her expertise in bringing Swampy to national notoriety when evicting him from the A30 Honiton Bypass in Devon in the late 1990s, creating a negative national view of environmental protestors. Although no one could genuinely substantiate Webster's involvement, such information, that I always researched more for myself, left me open-minded to the possibility of manipulation by the authorities, because only a professional could conjure up the discourse in this way.

Soon after this, I realised that the local media rag the Manchester Evening News, were very quick to release articles when it was condemning the camp but rarely shared a positive story. Rarely was anyone filmed for a mainstream media interview on live television, unless it was someone they had interviewed before. The non-live interviews broadcasted were always edited, so if the editor wanted a particular angle, they would speak to as many people as possible until they got the right quote to back up their narrative. Their discourse was usually presented in a certain light to reflect badly on the campaigners. So, where a viewer might have agreed with the protestor speaking initially, they now start questioning their judgement, thinking they are wrong. The only balanced journalism appeared in the Salford Star; their reporter Steve Speed would regularly come to the camp to find out more about this local issue for local people, whilst photographing and reporting events.

But the mainstream media bias we witnessed is gaslighting on a national scale, with all outlets playing their part, as directed by their neoliberal executives. This isn't conspiracy theory. It's not hard to find out that every fabric of society follows a neoliberal agenda, from the top down. Neoliberalism, or free market capitalism, which I was learning about in my undergraduate studies, began in the Thatcher and Reagan era of the 1980s. It is generally associated with privatisation, deregulation, globalisation, and austerity. At the end of the Cold War, the World Bank, and the International Monetary Fund (IMF) became more powerful, so they imposed these strict ideological policies on developing countries, weakening the role of those governments. Globally, it means an increased role of the private sector in society, especially in Western capitalist states' policy making. Even people in favour of capitalism, see neoliberalism as capitalism on steroids, with no social conscience. Profit before people appears to be the unwritten ethos that I could now see playing out in front of me.

Those of us at the bottom of this hierarchical system have little voice in the mainstream media unless you stand your ground and threaten reporters with no story. No malice is directed towards the reporter because they are just following orders; the corruption always comes from way up high. Realising these facts, I knew that change would never come from watching the 'news' because no real critical analysis took place. From then on, I decided not to have a TV and have not since. I question everything, particularly the common narrative from the status quo.

Barton Moss Solidarity Day
A week after 'flaregate', on the twelfth of January, we held one of the biggest national anti-fracking solidarity days ever seen, without the need for mainstream news publicity or even the help of Non-Governmental Organisations (NGOs) such as FoE or Greenpeace. Months earlier, I would have not believed it was possible without

either of their support. The Trades Council had some involvement in getting numbers, which was welcomed. But I soon learnt that when organising a campaign on a local issue, grassroots local organisation is more beneficial because people have a connection to their own environment and culture, and want to protect it.

That's not to say that outside help wasn't gratefully received. Kenny and Ross of Truthferret films from Brighton played a major part, so did Ian Crane, amongst others who travelled up and down the country to support the fight. Working together, the camp and members of the local community, strategically planned and prepared for all the events we held. We created and printed flyers, paid for by camp funds raised by the local community, and in the run up to the events, would spend up to four hours a day standing outside the local Tesco with camp members including Diane Steels, Boris Roscin and Shaun handing out the flyers. Our target audience was the wider local community because they would have to protect the precious mosses with us over the coming months and continue long after we had gone.

We worked long hours in this period, protesting, planning, leafletting, then protesting again before dinner. At the same time, other anti-fracking groups were being created every week in other places also under threat from the oil and gas industry. Daily livestream evidence of injustices coming directly from grassroot campaigners on the front lines would be broadcast on our computers and phones. More and more people were waking up to what was going on and were getting involved in stopping it. So, we also used social media to promote the solidarity day nationally, in the hope that busloads of supporters would come to us as they had done to Balcombe the summer before.

Our hard work was rewarded, because people came from all over the UK to show solidarity. With banners and costumes, children and music, it had the festival feel we had hoped for. Everyone was there in high spirits, bringing the morale boost we all needed, especially camp members because of what we were facing daily. Meeting many passionate, dedicated, and brave people from anti-fracking groups around the UK made the day unforgettable and will stay in my heart and mind forever. This day gave me the spiritual power and psychological strength to get through what I was about to face in the coming weeks and years ahead. The day concluded with the song 'Something Inside So Strong' sung by a local guy called Marcus, and joined in by the massive crowd assembled, before we all walked to the site gates.

That solidarity day I did not see one single police officer until most visitors had gone home, then, as if by a strange coincidence they returned. From then on, it felt like the police had created their legitimacy to overthrow the protest, once and for all. They were clearly not happy with the protest's growth and their failed 'flaregate' discourse.

In the early weeks of 2014, I witnessed some of the worst daily policing of demonstrations I have ever seen. On days when the local or national press came, which was rare, the police would conveniently back off, allowing us our protest peacefully and calmly, but the next day they would revert straight back to their aggressive bullying tactics. Then, campaigners would face knuckles ground in their backs, heels roughly stepped on, and women even said they'd been touched, groped and pressed up against. Either the peaceful and calm days were lulling us into a false sense of security in preparation for the next violent day or they were short of officers.

Lorry Surfing
One morning in late January, we were waiting at the top of Barton Moss Road as usual, when suddenly a Sky News van and reporters appeared. At the time, David Cameron was Prime Minister, and he had just announced a thirty-million-pound investment deal with Total, the French company involved in shale gas at an IGas site in Lincolnshire. We were the only front line against the industry in England at the time, so perhaps they wanted our opinion on the news.

When Cameron announced this big investment, that morning, the share price had surged. But by late afternoon it was already starting to fall. Throughout the Barton Moss campaign, the share price reached a 139.2 high, the day Cameron made the announcement. But, after twelve-months, the price was 25.0, dropping further, before the company formed new shares. It crossed my mind that maybe this was another part of the plan with fracking; to embezzle investors, most of whom I'm sure were Conservatives themselves, because exploratory wells were more often than not situated in Tory strongholds. These thoughts seemed logical because I could see no benefits to fracking or exploratory boreholes, for that matter.

During this time, the Conservatives were making announcements regularly in support of the industry. Articles about Cameron and then Chancellor of the Exchequer George Osbourne in the Telegraph or the Times telling their readers they were 'all out for shale' would doubtless persuade many to invest. Of course, those involved, would know about any announcement beforehand, to buy shares early. Was this why the neoliberal press was keen to broadcast the story? It all seemed like such a scam, I couldn't help be suspicious of the media's motive for being there.

That morning the convoy of lorries divided, whether strategically, or held up in traffic, in which case they could join the convoy further down the footpath. The first convoy involved three lorries, two from a company called Total Environmental Solutions. The two 'Total' companies were not linked in any way, as this company present were only used to remove excess water from the site, uncanny though.

Anyway, one moment I am chatting with a campaigner Theo Simon, who had arrived the night before, the next he has jumped up on top of one of the stationary lorries, to do a form of peaceful protest called lorry surfing. A second lorry roof also suddenly had a campaigner on its top, by another now sadly passed friend who went by the name of Lardo Fumblefoot, a resident on camp with his Druid partner Guinevere. Theo, a djembe drummer and singer in the folk music group Seize the Day, had been an environmental campaigner for many years. Now, here he was sitting on top of the lorry playing his drums.

While we were all enjoying the lorry occupations, the police tried to force the second convoy of trucks down the footpath at breakneck speed, trying to catch everyone off guard, breaking all traffic management plans in the process. I tried to get in front of one of the lorries to slow-walk, when two police officers rugby-tackled me to the ground. I landed an inch away from the side of the speeding lorry, which was now live on Sky News. (I later watched this video clip, in its entirety on the Sky News page, reliving how scary it was, but the beginning of the dangerous incident ended up being edited out, some time later.)

Shocked but undeterred, I jumped up to get in front of the next lorry before being pushed against a fence, yet still not arrested. The police had lost all control and were endangering people's lives by forcing lorries down a public footpath where people were gathered.

The traffic management plan was for lorries to head north past Barton Moss Road on the opposite carriageway, turn at a roundabout a quarter a mile further up, and then use the inside lane on the southbound carriageway. The traffic management plan was so trucks never turned right from the far carriageway across the nearside carriageway, because it was a busy dual carriageway. Yet now, just that had happened, with almost fatal consequences. That day, the commanding officer showed total disregard for the campaigners' safety, many from the local community, when they should have been facilitating our peaceful protest. Which commanding officer's decision was this?

February had now arrived, and I had planned to continue with my studies with an environmental science module. However, reading through the material, I decided it was not for me and that I was more suited to environmental policy modules, which freed me up until the autumn. Nevertheless, I'd already decided that I would study on camp in the evenings, and go home more frequently for typing up assignments, as I was now captivated by the protests. Plus, I felt protective of the people there, standing up against any undesirables that came the camp from time to time and keeping a close eye on the police.

By now, I'd upgraded my tent to a six-man, so I had a table and even carpet inside. I'd come a long way since that train ride to Irlam in November. Living there almost continuously for two-months and being part of the backbone of the campaign there, doing slow walks nearly every day, I've no doubt I was noticed by intelligence now. Still, the injustices I saw daily drove my determination to continue to stand up against industry by all peaceful means available.

It was all worth it, to see the likes of eighty-two-year-old Anne Power, who attended the protests most days. Exercising her right to protest, Anne was a real nuisance to GMP because they could not shove her around like they did other campaigners during slow-walks. Anne had quite a following around the country for her steadfast resilience to exercise her right under extreme circumstances.

Apart from when we were gathered every morning at the top of Barton Moss Road, and were visible to passing traffic, the rest of the protest was out of sight down the public footpath. The police were able to get away with whatever they chose, especially as all the local media, especially the MEN, were mostly silent to protestor concerns while continuing a disinformation campaign against us whenever they were required to do so.

Five

Start of the Right to Protest Denial

MY FIRST OF what was to be numerous protest-related arrests, took place on the ninth of February 2014, the evening before I had planned to take part in a sit-down obstruction at the top of Barton Moss Road and be arrested anyway. Had a camp member informed the police of what I had planned the next day? With many new faces coming and going, I often wondered if the camp had been infiltrated by undercover police, as had happened with many protest groups in the past.

Most evenings, we would gather outside the gates to the site at six-thirty to wait for the drilling rig workers' shift change. Usually, the police would simply facilitate our attempt to slow-walk the rig workers' minibus out of the drilling site. But this particular evening, the police had no intention of allowing protest and focused, instead, on arresting me. It was very unusual to see more than one high-ranking officer at these evening protests, yet there were four-sergeants in attendance.

From the start of the gathering outside the gates, I was targeted by one particular female officer. The vehicles then began leaving the site, heading in the opposite direction from camp over the motorway bridge. Turning left heading down from th bridge, this female officer pushed and shoved me into a wooden fence, directly at the side of the motorway, goading me for a reaction. I shouted in protest at being shoved and then I had about eight officers dive on me, trying to arrest me unlawfully. I resisted, struggling out of their grip and asking them what they thought they were doing. After a few minutes of resistance, I was arrested on outrageous charges of obstructing police and resisting arrest, and taken to the police station cells for a couple of hours.

The court at trial on the second of June 2014 found me not guilty of all offences because I was unlawfully detained in the first place, as I had been the one assaulted by police while exercising my right to protest. Of course, violent arrests such as mine would most likely have the effect of scaring people away, but by now I was used to seeing police violence, so it never deterred me. Not even the night after this first aggressive arrest.

I was bailed away from the main camp and the satellite camp we had set up weeks earlier for Big Dan who was given similar strategic restrictions, designed to reduce numbers able to participate fully in the protest. This was more likely the reason for my arrest. This camp was situated on the other side of the motorway in woodlands, but still within the Salford Mosses. It was on the route that smaller vehicles, but not lorries, could take from the drill site and the one the vehicles were trying to take this evening.

Released from the police station, I quickly set up a night camp outside the geographical bail zone, enabling me to stay nearby until morning, so I could still take part in the planned protest, even though I knew my participation would be short-lived because of my bail restrictions. I had chosen this upcoming action to be my first arrest after all, and nothing and no one was going to stop me from doing it, even if it was now to be my second arrest in less than twenty-four hours.

I was joined by Brown, Ian Tushingham and David Porter for the action, and from the start it was good fun. Protestors are very creative and usually have a wicked sense of humour. We made T-shirts for the occasion over the weekend, with the 'Footpath Protection Team' painted across the front and back. The slogans had two aims, one to ridicule the police for their months of illegal arrests on the footpath, they had been claiming was a highway, but also for the benefit of any photos shown in court, if it ever got that far. The entrance to the road where we chose to sit made this controversial detail clear, as did the 'public footpath' sign at different points along this single-track road. We made sure the footpath sign was in all pictures taken by our photographers and live streamers as we conducted our sit-down protest, which lasted around an hour in total. I was the first person arrested because of my breach of bail conditions.

Astoundingly, one day previously, a police officer was caught on camera by a campaigner, taking a public footpath sign down on this same footpath and putting it in the back of their van. The police had been using allegations of us blocking the 'highway' to arrest people illegally, as we had every right to be on a 'footpath', and we knew the difference in the eyes of the law. Was this Silver Commander Mark Robert's decision? What about Amanda Webster? Or was it someone else? Whoever was directing it, I had never witnessed this kind of blatant police obfuscation before, nor their total lack of respect for civil liberties. All Obstruction of the Highway arrests previously were unlawful and GMP commanders knew it, but it never deterred them.

I was reasonably confident the police would arrest me on charges of obstruction of the highway. However, I also knew, within forty-eight hours, the camp's lawyers would confirm that Barton Moss Road was indeed a public footpath; therefore the Crown Prosecution Service (CPS) had no realistic chance of obtaining a conviction. It was a classic case of you waste our time, and we will waste yours; and in this scenario we were the experts in wasting time, not them. However, we had got to a point where we had to be smart when using our 'arrest credits' because the police were just abusing the whole process. None of us original campaigners at the site could survive the duration at this rate of unlawful arrests. We would all soon be bailed away from the area entirely or remanded in prison, with no chance of conviction.

I was indeed charged with obstruction of the highway. The police were not aggressive this day, they politely asked us to remove or be arrested and we politely refused. However, I knew they would have to take me to a Magistrate's Court after a short time in the police station because I had broken bail. The other three would all be released with the same draconian bail conditions I had received the night before. For me, another key reason to take part in the protest was to be arrested again because I knew police were acting in an extreme manner, and I wanted to see if the Magistrate Courts would remove my restrictive bail conditions from the previous night, as I suspected they might.

The courts I found myself in that same afternoon were used to dealing with criminals every day, not peaceful protestors. Without much thought, the magistrates removed my restrictive bail conditions, opening the process up for anyone else arrested to apply directly to the courts, to have their restrictions removed as soon as they could get a solicitor to arrange a bail hearing. This way, no one had to wait for weeks to attend the far-off date the police deliberately chose with the aim of eradicating our protest and not face being remanded in prison. So now, rather than the protest failing with everyone bailed away from the site, people could now apply to the courts and have the conditions removed within a week. It felt good to have the law on our side and stick two fingers up to the corrupt police commanding officers.

Soon after, the CPS, by order of one of the three Manchester District Judges overseeing cases, was told to stop handing out these ludicrously draconian, geographical bail conditions. This esteemed Judge said it was wasting court time and taxpayer money, something the police were experts in at Barton Moss.

I certainly welcomed the Judge's recommendations, and had no intention of restricting my protest to protect the environment simply because of these strategic police decisions. Yet here I was, after spending almost three months without arrest, taken away in a police van twice in less than fifteen hours. I had been in police cells before, so the experience was made much easier, and in any case, once arrested no point arguing. I knew they were trying to intimidate me, but it would take more than this to make me leave this protest. Myself and Tush's case collapsed on the morning of the later trial and Foxy and Elmo were both found not guilty, after the police tried to change their charges.

Sometimes, however, doubts about whether I was doing the right thing did creep in, especially now I was getting hassle from the police. But the chance to go to Brussels for the Shale Gas World Conference on the twenty-first of February on behalf of the anti-fracking campaign, completely reaffirmed I was right to oppose this dirty industry. It was the first time I had travelled on my own in recovery, and I was quite anxious about it. Arriving in the strange city the day before the conference, I met up with another anti-fracking activist from Ireland, living in Brussels, for a few drinks, which helped me relax. Unfortunately, she could not make the conference the next day, but I was meeting up with some activists from Romania at the event.

Looking every bit the smart, suited delegate for the industry, I slipped into the event and watched, aghast, at the presentations extolling the benefits of shale. One slide in particular scared the hell out of me: it said 'all wells fail eventually', because of an engineering problem with the cement casing. *All wells.* I knew for absolute certain the industry had to be stopped at all costs and felt the importance of being a grassroots campaigner on the ground, slowing their operations down and sharing as much information as possible.

By March, what started out in November as a good couple of hours protest, slow-walking the lorries into the drilling site, was being aggressively hastened along by the police to no more than fifteen-minutes. During this period, another violent arrest took place on Vanda, a long-standing, female camp resident. What we witnessed and the shocking images that came later, showed how the TAU enjoyed aggressively manhandling her, while they cuffed her on the floor. We knew we had to step up our actions and take a new approach if we were to continue to be effective going forward, whilst halting the police violence.

One Friday afternoon, after a particularly rushed morning protest bringing the mood at the camp to a new low, two-activists dived out of a tent, flung themselves in the footpath and joined their arms together in a 'lock-on'. I'd never seen this method of protest up close before. A lock-on is a longer-lasting method of obstruction than a sit-in, as those involved place their arms down a length of pipe and lock-on to a device in the middle so they cannot be easily removed. The police have to get a specialist cutting team to come and safely extricate the protestors from the device before arresting them, which can take a few hours. The speed at which it all happened left the police shocked and angry, but what could they expect after the continual denial of lawful protest?

Jubilant from the action's effectiveness, the camp spent the weekend planning and preparing for the following week of similar direct actions. I had four devices made, with camp funds, for what was to be a four-way lock-on with three other campaigners at the camp. The pipes were made out of plastic but surrounded with mesh and tape to slow down the cutting team even more as they tried to get us all out. I knew this first direct-action of mine was sure to have me bailed away from camp, but I decided I had to do it and face those consequences. I was not prepared to camp at the side of road, day in day out, whilst being denied my right to protest by the police. We had to make sure these actions got local and national attention and had a massive impact on the fracking industry and the policing of the protest. All the actions that followed that week involved Barton Moss camp protestors, with many locals heading over for support.

The Monday morning of our planned action, I woke up at six o' clock and opened my tent to a long line of public order police stretching through the camp. Suspicion struck me: was someone feeding information back to police? Or, did GMP simply expect more lock-ons after Friday's events, and not want to suffer the same surprise and bewilderment at our actions this week?

As well as watching our every move in the camp, there were also two pairs of police officers walking up and down the length of Barton Moss Road from the camp to the A57 and back. However, the size of Barton Moss Road meant there would still be plenty of opportunities for us to slip through their patrol and execute the action. Thankfully, the night before, we had loaded the devices in the back of a vehicle on camp to be confident of successful delivery.

Initially, the action involved four of us, but Big Dan bailed out last minute after knowing our activity's details, which just left the three of us. I phoned the person with the vehicle on camp and told them to set off, knowing this would give us plenty of time to set up before police had a chance to stop us. But we had to be stealthy and avoid suspicion. With plenty for the police to observe in the camp, and a laid-back attitude from those of us involved, the three of us were easily able to get the lock-on devices out the back of the car and attach our arms through them. We sat down, locked-on together, about eighty-metres down Barton Moss Road, from the A57, just as a pair of police spotted what was going on. Too late for them to do much about it, we grinned at the knowledge that we'd be here for a while. The week of lock-ons to halt the progress of the drilling site and denial of protest had begun.

Our action was named the 'Buzz Lightyear' protest because pictures taken from above of the three of us locked together in a triangle looked similar to the cartoon hero. We were happy to have done what we set out to achieve. It felt great doing a decisive action that the usual police couldn't do anything about. The cutting team eventually came, and were much more pleasant than the police we'd been used to. It was a delicate operation cutting us out of our devices, which took this expert team two hours to complete.

We purposefully set up Buzz Lightyear where it would be of minimal inconvenience to the local community. Only a few houses over the moss were impacted, but there was an alternative route, just not for lorries. A lady living at one of these had been against the protests for months, but she had just come on side after her young son had woken up with a nightmare that the earth was going to be cracked, after seeing the drill rig daily, to and from home. Her son's nightmare meant she then researched the industry for herself, rather than just listen to government and mainstream media, and she was apologetic to the camp over her months of ignorance of our reasons for protecting her land. In the end, she even wrote a letter to the High Court in support of the camp, when the landowner Peel Holdings was trying to evict it. It goes to show how people's views change with a bit more independent research into matters.

One by one, we were arrested and spent the afternoon in custody before being bailed away from the protests. After judges had told the police to stop wasting their time with arrests for obstruction of the highway, when it was a footpath, police were now charging us with aggravated trespass, even though our protest was peaceful and on a public right of way. It all seemed more about finding anything to stop us protesting. But I thought I'd take my chances with a criminal conviction, rather than have my right to protest denied.

Just as I had done on my previous arrests, I chose to break bail conditions the next morning, as I was again defending my right to protest. I had only ever been peaceful, and if it hadn't been for the aggressive and dangerous manner the police were using, I would not have needed to take direct action at all. So I stood around celebrating with others at the camp as the second lock-on of the week was taking place. Pretty swiftly, I was arrested again for breach of bail. I was ordered to stay in custody and was transported to Manchester Magistrates Court at lunchtime for the afternoon session. The judge refused to remove my bail conditions and almost placed me on remand in jail. Shocking when you consider we were having to protest in this way because of the denial of our right to protest in the first place. Furthermore, the other charges I was on bail for had no realistic chance of conviction. I felt, the courts were now treating people as guilty before trial.

Although I was unable to be present for the later direct actions that week, I watched on livestream every day, as each lock-on shut down operations at the site for many hours. It took the police between three and eight hours to cut each device open. The final device of the week, the police were unable to extricate, so they carefully moved campaigners to the side of the road. The whole week of direct action had been a great success, and had finally received a lot more attention from the surrounding community, who stepped up their support of the protest and continued the resistance for themselves, right until the end. All this happened without any help from NGOs, just solid working-class grassroots community resistance.

Thereafter, even the police backed off to an extent; they knew events would escalate if they tried those dangerous and aggressive tactics again. Over the length of the protest between November 2013 and May 2014, there were 231 arrests made, including my four (only one conviction), which I'm proud of. The cost to the taxpayer of policing the protest was £1.7 million, some £2.3 million less than the Balcombe protests. An example, that the Barton Moss grassroots protest was less expensive to police, over a longer period of time, than the Balcombe NGO led protest. The most important lessons I learned during this time was how useless the democratic system is for people protecting their local communities from harm; and that no mainstream NGO would help when the lorries came rolling in. FoE only attended Barton Moss once throughout that whole time, and refused to participate in the slow-walk protest, physically turning their backs on events.

Learning more about NGOs as part of my studies, and experiencing their lack of involvement here, completely changed my opinion of them. Previously, I had believed these organisations were beneficial because it looks at first glance as if they are. But there's more to them than meets the eye. The international development NGO industry has risen from about 200 organisations in the late 19th century, to approximately 50,000 by 2010, rising exponentially since the 1970s along with free market capitalism. Crucially, while these organisations raise some money from public donations, they have become increasingly dependent on government funding. This raises important questions about whether these NGOs have become more concerned with money and protecting thousands of jobs, whilst limiting the critical tone of campaign messages. Many experts believe that neoliberalism, racism, and class issues are still at the core of these organisations because the environment is often involved in trade deals, generally at the expense of low-to-middle-income countries, poorer communities and business-as-usual politics.

It all perturbed me but it was time to move on after throwing myself in at the deep end. I would carry on researching the vast and fascinating subject of the environmental protest movement, NGOs and geopolitics, and take everything I learned and witnessed here into further action elsewhere.

Six

Setting up Community Camps for Other Communities in the UK

AFTER ALL THIS intense action, I needed a rest from anti-fracking protests, so spent some time in the South of England and South Wales with Vanessa Vine, whom I had met at one of the solidarity days at Barton Moss. Vanessa lived in a beautiful village in West Sussex, four miles from Balcombe, and was playing a central role in resistance to Cuadrilla. The warm southern spring weather was a welcome break from the four months of wind and rain I had just encountered.

During this time, Dart Energy targeted an area called Farndon in Cheshire. Elmo, who I'd become good friends with at Barton Moss, headed there to help the community resistance and wanted me to join him, but I desperately needed some recuperation. Nevertheless, I kept in contact with him about it. The drilling operation at Farndon was exploring the possibility of Coal Bed Methane (CBM) extraction. They were using a drilling rig from a company called Marriott Drilling in North East Derbyshire. Through Elmo, I got speaking to others from a local group near Chester, several miles from Farndon. They were already opposing IGas who had another Petroleum Exploration Drilling License (PEDL) for exploratory drilling in Upton, near Chester.

A few weeks later, in April 2014, my resistance to the fracking industry took me to Upton. This time I would be part of a team which occupied the area designated for another drilling rig from the same fracking company that I had opposed at Barton Moss. Just after midnight, a group of us dived out of vans stocked with metal mesh heras fencing and put a Section Six notice on an area around the gate entrance to the field. This process involves taking possession of land and quickly erecting a structure, so occupants cannot be removed without implementing the Prevention of Illegal Eviction from Unlawful Occupation of Land Act. This means only a landowner could have us removed through a court order. This occupation was the first time a field designated for exploratory drilling had been occupied.

As with all the other discourse with the fracking industry, landowners were not always aware of the whole process of exploratory drilling or oil and gas extraction when they signed agreements (usually twenty-five years) with drilling companies. But with our presence raising awareness they would surely research more. It was expecially important to occupy land near the drilling site when the landowner's community were strongly opposed to the industry. So just maybe we were doing him a favour.

We had already had conversations with locals, just as others had at Barton Moss, and they had decided our land occupation needed to be the next step in their community resistance. However, as soon as dawn broke, we had the local police outside the camp asking us about our plans. Our intentions were no different from those we had set out to achieve at Barton Moss – to slow the industry down and build a wider grassroots resistance.

Throughout the day, local people came and brought tea, coffee, milk, food and materials, just as happened at Barton Moss. The community came together as a social hub, and there was always a constant presence of people who lived in the area supporting and staying on camp in the early weeks and months. I set out to build the kitchen with pallets and timber delivered and paid for by locals, using a similar template to the one I had helped create at Barton Moss. I planned to lay the cornerstone for the community hub and move on.

Soon after, the landowner and camp agreed to keep as much space as possible accessible to the farmer for animal grazing.

At this time, there was a ramping up of the threat of the fracking industry all across the country, and other vulnerable communities needed the same resistance expertise that we had learned over the last six-months. I was ready to share all I knew with however many groups I could reach, to empower them to resist this abhorrent industry. So, I only stayed at Upton camp for two weeks before moving on to help campaigners in another two areas also under threat in East Yorkshire.

By coincidence, or more likely tactics, that spring of 2014, Mark Roberts also began work in Cheshire. He had taken his position as Assistant Chief Constable at Cheshire Constabulary, where he became National Lead for Football Policing and, more importantly, Regional Lead on Public Order Policing.

As well as stopping any imminent drilling in that Upton field, it was also an ideal location for activists to rest from the intensity of the still ongoing protest at Barton Moss, whilst also having somewhere to stay if bailed away from that protest, just twenty-five miles away. Over the next eighteen months, I would visit Upton occasionally, for a short stay, as it was closer to home while I was studying.

The camp was evicted in January 2016 but in managing to resist the development of IGas, it was one of the most successful blockades ever in the anti-fracking campaign. I believe the success was down the relationship between the community and the camp, apart from one individual Fargo McCann, who tried to divide camp and community. I will discuss McCann more later because this was not the only place where he tried to divide community members and activists. The camp eviction and the events leading up to it I will also revisit in more detail later. My next destination was across the Pennines in East Yorkshire.

Set at the Southern tip of the beautiful Yorkshire Wolds just a few miles west of the town of Beverley, is a place called Walkington, and a few miles south east of Beverley, a village called Marton. On the edge of each of these villages, an exploratory borehole was drilled in a field by an energy company called Rathlin Energy Ltd, a wholly-owned subsidiary of Connaught Oil & Gas Ltd, a private company office in Calgary, Canada. The drilling of these exploratory boreholes at

Crawberry Hill, near Walkington and West Newton, near Marton occurred in the second and third quarter of 2013, respectively. At the time, a man called David Montagu-Smith was the chairman of Rathlin Energy, who was also the chair of the Campaign to Protect Rural England (CPRE) in the Northamptonshire West district. I was astounded to know a chairman of a fracking company, was also a chair of protecting Rural England. Locals informed us that Rathlin was about to do a fracking test at one or both sites, but they were unsure which site would be first.

Shaun, one of the first front line campaigners at Barton Moss, and I took a trip over to decide which site we should choose to start a protection camp outside. First, we went to Marton, a tiny, rural village, miles from anywhere, with not even a local shop. The first thing I noticed as we came through the village was a police dog unit vehicle on a driveway, which had a 'for sale' sign outside.

I instantly thought: *here we have the police pretending to be a private security firm for the industry, giving themselves time to get out before the fracking starts and their house price drops in value, all the while saying they are a neutral force.*

My next observation, which I found quite funny, albeit troubling, was that next-door-but-one was also for sale. Maybe they never spoke to the neighbour in between so they had no idea what fracking meant for their house price, let alone the community as a whole.

Anyway, we met Pippa King and another campaigner called Kirsty, who both lived in Hull, had a look at the drill site and the surrounding area before heading off to Walkington eight miles away. The ancient parish of Walkington is a beautiful village, with a shop and three pubs, in one of the most sought-after communities to reside in East Yorkshire. Initially, we could not locate the drilling site, so we stopped and asked a Walkington resident if they knew of its location, unsure how many locals even knew it existed.

However, in perfect synchronicity, we stopped to ask a lady who happened to be one of the original founding members of the local campaign group against Rathlin's plans before Rathlin had drilled the exploration well years earlier. She directed us to the site, situated over a mile outside the village, near a geographical point called Crawberry

Hill. The drilling site's surrounding environment was exposed but beautifully rural. The grass verges alongside the road around the exploratory compound were some four feet high. Twelve-foot hedges lined the fields and verge, the habitats of a chorus of wildlife about to be severely disrupted, and even displaced, by a noisy, destructive industry.

We decided on West Newton, near Marton for the first protection camp. We told Pippa and headed back to Upton. Pippa King I admired and am still friends with, does much work on dangers of facial recognition (biometrics). I trusted her. The other person Kirsty I was unsure of, but remembered her from her days at the Barton Moss camp, when she made reference to her army background and being involved with the Occupy movement.

After Shaun and I had more time to assimilate our decision, on our way back to Chester, we changed our minds. We decided that Crawberry Hill was actually the best location logistically, but decided to tell no one we had changed our plans. We knew if we had chosen wrong, we only had a short distance to relocate, which was fairly straightforward.

At the same time, a camp and protest were also underway at Daneshill in North Nottinghamshire. The campaigners had been there for many weeks resisting the exploration of coal bed methane by the same company from Farndon, Dart Energy. I had chosen not to go there because I'd been told there were members of Occupy involved, which throughout the Barton Moss protests, I had heard troubling stories of some of its members. This Daneshill protest was the first time I had heard of *managed protest*; where those present at Daneshill agreed with police that lorries would sit outside parked up for two hours and no more.

My Occupy suspicions were later backed up by evidence gleaned on research, including a lead case law judgement from the Occupy London Stock Exchange (LSX) protests, another managed protest. The Occupy movement had taken possession of land next to St Paul's Cathedral in London in October 2011, alledgedly as a protest against the political elites choosing to, "protect corporations, financial institutions and the rich at the expense of the majority." At its peak there were some two-hundred tents on public land predominantly owned by the City of London. However, after two months of occupation, on the eighteenth of January 2012 the City of London successfully obtained an order for possession of the public highway and an injunction against current and possible protestors on the land in a High Court judgement, known as City of London V Samede and others. Samede is the same person, who was friendly with Brown at Barton Moss and close friends with Tina Rothery, who visted weekly from Lancashire. Justice Lindblom, had considered protestor rights under Articles 10 and 11 of the European Convention for Human Rights (ECHR), the right to freedom of expression and freedom of association, on balance with the City of London's rights to assert property rights and to enforce compliance with statutes regarding public property.

On the twenty-second of February 2012, the Court of Appeal of England and Wales delivered its judgment upholding this decision in the lower court. The court then unanimously rejected the right to appeal their decision. Therefore, the judgement became restrictive to Articles 10 and 11 of the ECHR for obstruction and interference of the highway on public land, and was still leading case law in England and Wales. Case law means Judges making future decisions in public highway cases, take the wording of that ruling as influential in the decision making process, because many legal arguments have already been explored. Nevertheless, I knew many camp residents at Daneshill, were there to protect the environment and were supported by their local group Frack Free Nottinghamshire.

The morning before we set off for East Yorkshire, we got word that some of these campaigners at Daneshill were now heading to the West Newton site near Marton, in what we believed was an attempt to arrive before us. This rapid movement made me suspicious because only two people thought we were heading to that location, and one of them was an Occupy member. As planned, we headed to Crawberry Hill and formed the protection camp there. There was a conflict at first because the people who set up at West Newton were trying to get both camps to join together, but we were quite happy with two, because we could now monitor both drilling sites.

Seven

Protection Camp and Community Working Together

AFTER SPENDING DECADES with depression, walking around looking at the floor, I now held my head high and saw the beauty of nature all around me, in all its splendid glory. That late spring afternoon, the weather was beautiful; we could have been abroad and not got a better suntan. The night sky was equally impressive, with no light pollution for miles and very few vehicles passing on that high road above the village of Walkington. It was a stunning location, which I felt honoured to be protecting, even if some people were unaware why we were there or didn't want us around.

With a niggling awareness that everyone was not always who they claimed to be, I nevertheless met some fabulous campaigners in the following weeks and months, including, amongst others, Jon and Val Mager. Green Party members at the time, who lived in Beverley, they had heard about the forming of the Crawberry Hill camp and came to visit virtually every day from the start. Val was a semi-retired artist, and Jon was the retired Director of Adult and Children's Services. We would also be joined most days by other retired locals, nicknamed 'geriactivists' by other community members, a moniker most of them weren't too keen on. Their age range at the time was from sixty-four to eighty-four, so it was always a laugh when people drove by shouting, "Get a job!" The former and current professional roles of people there included senior probation officer, librarian, headteacher, teacher, scientist who worked for the NASA space shuttle programme, university professor, university lecturer, senior executive and tai chi teacher.

I realised that people from right across the social, political and philosophical spectrum were coming together for this campaign. I met different people every day who I would not have had the pleasure of meeting if I was not campaigning on this issue. Many East Yorkshire residents deserve mention for their kindness, generosity and unwavering support include Mike and Ann Brookes, Peter and Sue Dack, Judy Dickinson, Mike Farman, Wendy Cross, Sue Weaver, and Rhona Johnston.

The first day of Rathlin's attempt to work on-site, a camp protestor who had resided at Barton Moss and Upton called Ben Deevoy, blocked the drill site at Crawberry Hill. Unbelievably, a tractor driver for the landowner, Ellerington, drove into him at a slow speed, knocking him to the floor. We often found some landowners hostile to campaigners, but I put that down to them taking the money from the frackers and not wanting our presence alerting the community to what was unfolding.

To try and calm the atmosphere, Jon and Val began a peaceful protest at the side of the gates. Val stood and explained why, as locals, they were registering their objections and supporting the camp. Jon sat and meditated. But after about fifteen minutes, they were both arrested, under the Trade Union and Industrial Relations Act, and taken by police to the Humberside police custody suite. Here, the police tried to persuade them to plead guilty, which they refused. The Act is really aimed at Trade Union pickets. Val and Jon were charged with intimidating the driver sent to replace the first tractor driver.

For the next six hours, a few of us waited outside the custody suite for them, and were there as a welcoming party when they were released just before midnight. As campaigners, we never allowed anyone arrested to leave a police station without being greeted by fellow protestors, there in solidarity. Arrestee support was always organised; it happened daily outside Swinton police station during the Barton Moss protests, and was always a welcome and heart-warming action. It was an unwritten rule to never leave a comrade behind in battle - and we were undoubtedly in battle now, against the industry and the police.

Humberside Police shamefully showed from the very start of this campaign how it would deny the rights of the local community to peacefully protest. Jon and Val were both bailed away from the area around the drilling site, even though they lived in Beverley, and Val was born in East Yorkshire. Of course, neither stayed on camp, but their expertise against Rathlin's plans was a constant annoyance to Rathlin and East Riding of Yorkshire Council (ERYC) for the duration after that. So, although Humberside Police thought they were being clever, all they achieved was the generation of increased interest and support from the wider community. The Crown Prosecution Service (CPS) wisely dropped the case against both of them later.

A week or two later, Total Environmental Solutions whose lorries attended Barton Moss, needed access to drain the surface water from the ditches around the drilling pad, which was awash with drowned wildlife. There was no Guantanamo Bay-style security around the Crawberry Hill site, as was the case at Barton Moss, just five-foot stakes with barbed wire linking stakes together all around the area. This sudden appearance of lorries alarmed us: we thought this might be the beginning of works on the site.

During the following days, we decided to build a tower of pallets in front of the gates as a symbol of defiance and a lookout for lorries and police presence. This structure was the first anti-fracking tower built outside a drilling site, and other protest camps would later follow suit. As the police had already warned we would be denied protest, we were left with little choice but to build the barricades.

With the wider community aware of our presence, they were starting to ask questions of their local representatives. Therefore, a meeting was held in the Dog and Duck public house back room with parish council members, community representatives and campaigners. I was invited along to talk about the protestors' side of things. Although I now rarely drank, when I would go off camp I sometimes had a few pints of Guinness. So, before I went through to the meeting, I went the bar to order myself a pint. The Dog and Duck wasn't the biggest of pubs and it was very busy. As I arrived at the bar, a man in his late thirties to early forties asked if I was living on the camp.

"Yes, I am," I said.

"What can I do to help?" he asked.

"Join us in slowing the lorries – and the industry – down and protecting your family's beautiful, natural environment," I said, not caring who he was. I was proud of what I did, and we needed as many people as possible to help us.

"Ah, that might be difficult," he said, "I'm a police officer."

Unbelievable! I thought.

"Well, you'll be facing off with me daily then," I told him.

"No, I won't," he replied, "I've just taken three months leave."

I remembered the dog van at West Newton weeks earlier. Here was another innovative Humberside copper getting out before the shit hits the fan and community turn against him.

In one of those moments, where clarity hits you like lightening and changes everything from then on, I realised that local bobbies didn't police the protests in their local communities. It was always police drafted in from elsewhere or from the opposite side of the county. I remembered Vanessa Vine and others telling me that the Balcombe protests had police forces from the West Country. In fact, officers on the frontlines had often come from quite a distance away from the threatened community, so they would have no attachments to the people they were forcing the government's will on.

Not only was the government rushing through a dangerous industry, they were also putting police officers in difficult situations. You can imagine the pressure on the police officer and his family in the community if he was to take part in such activities. One only knows how they must have felt enforcing the industry on another community. But I never had time for sympathies. Police officers are well aware of their commitments when they sign up and are paid to follow orders in most instances. Hence, why it is important to have referendums on such important issues, not just government imposing its will on the people, unchecked. For that is authoritarianism.

After this meeting, I hoped few more people would see our side, and research further for confirmation that what we were doing was not only justified, but something they might like to support or join. I do not know if that meeting made future decisions on where Rathlin would choose to start their fracking tests, but they were at least now aware this community was well-informed. Rathlin had previously been on the charm offensive, as these companies often do to insist the operation would be safe, which the mainstream narrative backed up with its biased view in favour of the development.

Walkington Public Meeting

On the nineteenth of May, a large public meeting in the village of Walkington took place, for the parish council to inform the wider community about what was going on at the drilling site, now that the camp's presence had alerted to them to the fact that something was happening. The village hall was packed out, with standing room only. Even the BBC were there outside, speaking to the public as they entered the event and recording what went on therein. I spoke on behalf of the camp again, with my aims directed at how the village could support us in disrupting the industry wherever possible and helping with water, wood and basic supplies. Of course, front line protesting is not for everyone, and each of us has our part to play, whatever that quality may be.

The majority of village politics is run by parish councils, which makes rafts of decisions on land development, upkeep of the civic space and are generally the first point of contact for community issues. Coming from a city, I'd experienced a different type of council, more about preserving green spaces, developing local amenities and creating a vision for the local area. In contrast, councils in the countryside appear more and more to be about allowing building and development all over great swathes of our stunning countryside, no matter if they completely destroy them. And it seemed that large landowners favoured this type of politics. So, I was none too keen on them, if I am honest.

Furthermore, Parish Councils have had an array of complex issues and bureaucracy to deal with, so there's not enough time or motivation for counsellors to research individual matters in depth. Add to that a media bias that more often than not portrays the narrative that we need the gas to heat our homes, and for a whole host of important things, not mentioning that the onshore oil extracted was for plastic production, adding to the environmental crisis. If this ever came up, these onshore oil and gas companies Public Relations (PR) would exert the importance of those plastic items to include food packaging, plastic bottles, polyester fibres, syringes and other medical supplies, essential for humanity to survive...on a planet they were about to destroy. You couldn't make it up.

In terms of energy use, it was much cheaper to get conventional gas resources from Europe, without any greater risk to our environment than polluting the water table, natural aquifers, air pollution and releasing potent greenhouse gasses like methane into the atmosphere. We aimed to get across that this is the reality of this industry, suggesting parishioners do some more research. When they did, they usually understood and joined us in whatever way they could, supporting camps with food and washing clothes; starting up websites and newsletters; and all the social media sharing. And if they wanted to, they were welcome to visit the camp, have a brew and a good, intellectual discussion.

I explained that our campaign's central aim was to share and educate the local community about what was happening in the area – and having a camp in the area under threat made this easier and attracted attention to the cause. It gave us the opportunity for the local community to question camp representatives in more detail. Armed with the facts, I could tell people were getting on-side.

Outside that meeting, the BBC interviewed three people for their evening news; two were saying we need to stop the industry. What a relief, our side finally put forward. Obviously, to keep it balanced they found one person in favour, spouting the need for gas to heat homes, in line with the mainstream narrative. For once, it wasn't a bad bit of journalism, at least it was presenting our views and knowledge, even if in tiny soundbites. I'm not a fan of the media, but I understood, for some, it was their only source of information. Could the truth at last be forcing its way out? Were the press finally presenting us 'eco-warriors' in a more favourable light?

One day, wanting another news story, a BBC reporter came to Crawberry Hill protection camp and after editing their footage, created a ridiculously biased piece against the campaigners. When they returned again the next day, we informed them that they would not be getting any more interviews if they didn't do a piece that told our story for balance. Thankfully, they did, but that's how radical one needed to get to receive a fair representation in the mainstream media.

All was quiet after these events at Walkington, so mid-June I decided to take some time off. The road alongside the camp had now closed completely to all traffic for overhead power cable works, which suggested nothing major would take place for at least two months on the drill site. Apart from a few weeks in Sussex and Pembrokeshire in spring, it had been nine months, full-on, high-intensity living. I needed a break, but I never stopped researching the wider green movement and questioning the narrative around climate change, which was being talked about and campaigned on more and more.

Eight

The Climate Change Movement

THE BIRTH OF the centralised international climate change movement in the UK began in earnest in September 2005, under the umbrella group Stop Climate Chaos, the same year as the G8 summit in Gleneagles. This organisation is a coalition of environmental and international development NGOs. Coincidentally, the Kyoto Protocol was also entered in to force earlier that year, which currently has 192 parties signed to the agreement. This Kyoto Protocol commits states to reduce greenhouse gas emissions based on a scientific consensus that global warming is driven by man-made CO_2 emissions. Based on the principle of common but differentiated responsibilities, it acknowledges combatting climate change is different between countries because of individual capabilities, owing to economic development. Therefore, it puts the majority of emphasis to reduce emissions on developed countries. Its reasoning behind this is that historically developed countries are responsible for current levels of emissions in the atmosphere.

In 2006, environmental activists who attended the Gleneagles event organised the first Climate Camp at Drax in Yorkshire, before scheduling two further in the following years - at the now long-standing Grow Heathrow camp and Kingsnorth coal-fired power station. These camps involved various green campaign groups, change agents and organisations with the purpose of drawing attention to carbon emitters whilst acting as a base for direct action and 'developing consensus ways' to create a zero-carbon society. All sounded fair enough environmentally and I had always thought NGOs were for the good. But my reasearch was showing that their work more often than not supported lucrative carbon-offsetting in the development sector, not the system change humanity needed to tackle climate change. These consensus ways coincided with a new established discourse earlier in that decade, of 'consensus and cooperation.' This discourse originally involved nuclear energy policy and public engagement, but had now spread to all energy-related policy matters, which included fracking. For some reason, these climate change agents appeared almost non-existent between 2008 and when the Climate Camp group officially disbanded in 2011 – just as the anti-fracking movement was starting to grow. Climate Camp's reason for scattering was to try 'new radical experiments to tackle the intertwined ecological, social and economic crisis'. This statement is signficant because I was soon to begin experiencing these radical experiments and for all the wrong reasons.

Local anti-fracking groups were soon being established, most notably Ribble Estuary Against Fracking (REAF), Residents Action on Fylde Fracking (RAFF), Roseacre Awareness Group (RAG) and Preson New Road Action Group (PNRAG), which eventually led to the umbrella group Frack Free Lancashire in 2015, founded by Bob Dennett and Ebony Johnson.

This time also saw the beginning of a different branch of activists, the climate change NGOs, becoming involved in the campaign against the industry. The two most high-profile NGOs in the UK are Friends of the Earth and Greenpeace, but they're only a small fraction of the environmental movement. FoE do have a network of local groups, while Greenpeace, which receives no government funding, has large private donations and celebrity supporters. However, private funding can benefit less controversial industries and middle-class concerns, including green consumerism, whilst marginalising more radical environmental issues, such as the storage of hazardous waste and social deprivation.

The different between light and dark green environmentalism

These international and national institutions are a combination of light and bright green environmentalists, who preach about individuals' private action, clean technologies to prevent pollution, and biotechnology undoing established environmental damage. Carbon off-setting is a classic example of a wider shift towards a norm of voluntary processes, policed by the providers themselves, based on principles and standards and not rules and regulations.

In contrast, they run counterproductive with a dark green shade of environmentalism, which believes civilisation is intrinsically damaging to the environment and needs drastic, systemic changes to become sustainable, illuminating the importance of the development of self-sufficient communities within a decentralised approach.

A key issue is that International Non-Governmental Organisation (INGOs) are increasingly tied to public service delivery and government agendas. Rather than advocating radical system change, they have adopted the role of policy innovators in many institutionalised settings. Hence, why it is important for communities to be free to protest on local issues, no matter how much of a nuisance that might be to some, just as countries in poorer parts of the world, should remain free to do so.

§

The organisation Frack Off appeared to be the first structured component of the Climate Camp that resurfaced, beginning their campaign against fracking in August 2011, with a banner drop from Blackpool Tower. In November, the same campaign group stormed Cuadrilla's drilling site and scaled the rig at another site in Banks, Lancashire, to drop another banner essentially highlighting the issue.

In October that same year, the Occupy London Stock Exchange protests took place, also involving elements of Climate Camp, which lead to the forming of Frack Off London, linking the Occupy movement with Frack Off.

In 2012, the quasi-campaign group No Dash for Gas was the next Climate Camp component to appear, targeting gas-fired powered stations, most notably their week-long occupation of EDF's West Burton plant in Nottingham in October 2012. A present-day element of the centralised group that originated from Climate Camp is RTP, founded late in 2012.

In May 2013, a Camp Frack 2 weekend was jointly organised by Frack Off and the Campaign Against Climate Change and held at Mere Brow near Southport. *Strange name for a camp against fracking, I thought, or was it against fracking?* Might it have been using the fracking industry as a radical experiment to further their climate change campaigning of zero-carbon on behalf of the lighter shade of green international organisations?

Camp Frack took place over three days in Singleton, with some three-hundred in attendance, mostly those pushing the agenda of climate change within the business-as-usual model of capitalist politics and organisations. However, knowledgeable local anti-fracking group called Ribble Estuary Against Fracking (REAF) was also involved, one of the country's first local grassroots anti-fracking groups. With all of these events and actions, there would always be decent, well-meaning, local campaigners working alongside NGO employees, seemingly fighting for the same cause. But were they?

Although Campaign Against Climate Change, in partnership with Frack Off, created this gathering, Stop Climate Chaos would have been the mother INGO for all information collected. That organisation had been the umbrella group for international climate change civil society organisations since 2005, of which the Campaign Against Climate Change, FoE and Greenpeace UK are members..

I was starting to see a distinct difference between grassroots campaigning against fracking and that of these third sector organisations. Many of the organisers of climate change events, even protests, are on the payroll of environmental NGOs and global institutions with powerful private backers wanting to keep business-as-usual with a light greenwashing to appear as if something's being done to protect our planet. Environmental NGO campaigns are primarily designed to influence supporters to sign petitions to change national policy – often in favour of light green consumerism.

My reason for outlining these corporate NGO organisations and the groups that materialise from them is an awareness that was growing of people acting on behalf of a climate change agenda, and the conflicting ideologies within the movement. It's not just a hunch, I've researched it until my eyes are sore. National NGO campaigners are not grassroots movements at all; they are change agents at the local level, to do the work of those at the international level, in changing local and national policies and minds on behalf of international institutions. This is not climate change denial, as I'm well aware the climate is changing, but a conflicting ideology of how we approach the matter within environmentalism. Climate NGOs focus on changing people's minds and behaviour, using the discourse of consensus and cooperation. In contrast, grassroots groups believe in disrupting unethical businesses, policy and protecting local environments.

This divide in environmental ideology later became a combatant theme within the anti-fracking campaign. I was firmly in the dark green environmentalist camp and found those campaigners with similar ethics more resilient in their determination to halt the fracking industry whilst being non-negotiable with the authorities. We didn't want business-as-usual, we wanted complete system change. But the powers that be, at the top of industry and finance don't want anything to change, least of all through the power of the people. Initially, this combatant theme confused me because those campaigning on climate change were declaring a state of emergency, so one would expect they'd welcome peaceful but radical support from all campaigners. But this was not the case.

Nine

The Industry Fighting Back
with Agents?

REJUVENATED AFTER MY holiday, I headed back to East Yorkshire to catch up on the Crawberry Hill campaign. Soon after, on the second of July 2014, a convoy of about sixty trucks and vans started rolling into West Newton with a major police escort. We were caught off-guard and there was no obstruction by camp residents as the trucks entered or on the lane approacjhing the site. We raced over from Crawberry Hill to witness the site equipment all in the compound, brought in by one big unobstructed convoy. Gutted. Freedom of movement was denied during the operation, so until the police operation was over, we were confined three-hundred-metres away from the site entrance.

Soon after, Rathlin Energy and the landowners of the sites were trying to obtain injunctions to stop both camps having any impact on their operations, forbidding protestors from being near the sites. So in July, Ian Crane and Jon Mager travelled south to the High Court in Fetters Lane, London, to dispute this possibility. To begin with, a duty lawyer attempted to bring both West Newton and Crawberry Hill camps together, which Ian refused, preferring them to be treated separately. And Jon wanted the hearing to take place in Hull because he believed it was a local issue. So there was dispute and push-back by us from the start.

The hearing went ahead anyway, and the Judge instructed the Crawberry Hill camp to remove the tower from the site entrance. The West Newton camp was allowed to stay because their representative, aka Joe Public, had agreed to work with the police more effectively. By more effectively, I mean managed protest, basically waving banners and not being an obstruction. Perfect, if you want to stand about drooling over the drilling operation, but it wasn't going to stop it. The court order was for us to dismantle and move the structure within thirty-five days. It was inevitable really, but there was no intention of removing it, so we knew eventually we would have a visit off the National Eviction Team (NET). The NET are protestor, squatter and traveller removal experts, seperate to police, formed in 1995 and a part of the High Court Enforcement Group.

During this hearing, the local community found out for the first time that Rathlin had a twenty-five-year lease with the landowners of both sites, with the option for a further twenty-five years. Hardly the short-term exploration that Rathlin had been claiming to appease the villagers. In fact, this was clear evidence of the long-term planned industrialisation of the countryside. Thanks to Crane and Mager reporting back, I realised that you discover much more factual information in the High Court hearings than you would otherwise know, so it's worth being there in person.

§

A couple of weeks later, a guy calling himself Logic Al turned up at Crawberry Hill, claiming to be an animal rights activist. *Interesting,* I thought, *that could bring another stream of protestors in.* But as always, I kept my distance from everyone until I knew a consistency in their life story, which required time. Not long after his arrival, the police spoke at a schools' conference in Yorkshire. Under the 'Prevent' banner, aimed at preventing extremist thinking in the community, and linked anti-fracking activists with animal rights activists. For the first time, we were categorised as domestic extremists. I thought, if we were domestic extremists, then the fracking companies were international terrorists.

In my nine months on the anti-fracking front line, travelling round different communities, nobody came across as an extremist. Was it extreme to want to protect the earth, water and air from further pollution and destruction? I also hadn't come across any animal rights activists among the crowds, so Logic Al's appearance seemed strange timing, just before being nationally linked with this group. But it's a mystery to me why animal rights activists are domestic terrorists too, when they're trying to save animals. Against the state and the status quo? You must be a domestic extremist.

So be it. I'd seen it coming. The 'flaregate' incident prepared me for almost any discourse or portrayal of us; the authorities would try and denounce the movement. Plus, I had to remind myself this was not a new movement; some people would have long-established positions in campaigns, all the way back to 2006. It was now 2014. Were the authorities that concerned about grassroot resistance that further agents and actors were needed on their behalf? From here on, I noticed more NGO involvement and strange cult-like behaviour.

Back at West Newton, the camp now had a new self-proclaimed leader, Louise Castro. No one knows where she came from, but we soon found out she was renting a house in Sproatley, a couple of miles from West Newton. Her residence in the area alarmed me because I would not rent a home in any area to then live at camp; what would be the point? I was further dumbfounded when I learned she was to continue working with the police on a protest that allowed no more than waving a banner outside the gates, facilitating a zero-tolerance policy on slow-walking demonstrations, which were lawful and practical. I never understood this stance. Why stand outside a drilling site if you were just going to watch the operation day in day out, without doing something constructive to slow it down? Of course, documenting what is happening on site was a needed cause of action, but that only required one or two people. At Crawberry Hill, most of the camp would use the slow-walking technique as our primary form of protest when the time arrived, as it was the only successful form of resistance that we had at our disposal, without taking direct action with lock-on devices. Why did the commanding officers not allow it here? Because they wanted us to fail. Whilst others had taken leave, so as not to be involved in policing any local protests.

The Crawberry camp and West Newton rarely seen eye-to-eye, which undoubtedly delighted the police and intelligence agencies. A group of us had decided a change in protest at West Newton was required, and it was more convenient if we camped nearby. There was no point joining the other camp, as they had a zero tolerance policy on slow-walking vehicles. There was only a small group of us, but we knew how to occupy a piece of field. In early July, we organised some building equipment and tents and managed to occupy a field at the bottom of the lane by West Newton. However, whilst heading back to Walkington for more equipment, the police turned up and were troubling those we had left behind holding the base for a short time, so we turned back. As we entered the field, we saw Castro loudly telling the police they had to move us. It was apparent she did not want the ineffective protest at West Newton to change. But the landowner had already accepted our presence, so there was nothing that could be done. Castro could not get the police to move us, no matter what she thought, so we finished setting up and stayed the night, knowing that the police couldn't remove us with our S6 notices everywhere.

Logic Al who had turned up at Crawberry Hill, was now staying at West Newton. He came down to our camp from the Castro-controlled base and tried to persuade us to sit back and wait until there were enough people to occupy the rig. Of course, if we wanted to occupy the rig that same evening, we could have, so I was puzzled by his proposition. Furthermore, why had they not already occupied the rig? After all, there were enough of them not doing anything very constructive, including Barton Moss campaigners Dunne and Tush. This discourse of suggesting people wait, as they had it under control, became a key tactic from some individuals in future protests. Regardless, I was suspicious of Logic's motives because it seemed he, like most on that camp, was allowing Rathlin to continue with their operations unchallenged. After all, they had been at that camp for many weeks and shown no resistance to Rathlin's operations. None of it made sense, only that it was an authoritarian, controlled camp.

The next morning, myself and Phil Whyte decided we would take action and slow-walk any vehicles that came or went from the site. Discussions with the police were blunt, they had a zero-tolerance to slow-walking, but we were doing it because it was a lawful protest, which we explained to the commanding officer present. After witnessing Jon and Val's wrongful arrest weeks earlier, I already knew that civil liberties were not something Humberside Police cared much about. So it didn't surprise me when, within ninety seconds of a starting the slow walk of vehicles leaving the site, the police waded in unlawfully arresting both of us and Tush who had joined us from the Castro controlled camp. There were two-riot-vans of police, with some eight to ten thugs between the two. I say thugs, because these coppers are what I describe as level one public order police, who thrive on intimidation and power, which is why they're promoted to these units. One minute I'm walking and the next I'm grabbed from behind and handcuffed. I didn't resist arrest, so I've no idea why I was handcuffed considering I was in a lane surrounded by pea fields, miles from anywhere. We were placed in a police van and driven away to a police station near Hull, were we spent many hours in custody.

After release from custody, our bail restrictions from a geographical space between and around the two drilling locations was about one hundred square miles in total, over half of Humberside. They were clearly following the draconian police tactics from Barton Moss to eradicate the protest – but this was taking it to the next level. Here we were, supported by East Yorkshire residents to protect their communities, while being denied by the very people paid to protect those residents, whilst one copper was selling up and another on leave because of the industry.

I kept to my bail conditions this time and did not get arrested the next day, because I still had one outstanding court case from Barton Moss. I applied to the courts in the interim period for a bail hearing, as I wanted my bail conditions removed as quickly as possible, just as I always did. At that hearing, a couple of weeks later on the twenty-third of July, yet again my bail restrictions were rightfully removed.

This freed me up to go back to West Newton, which I did straight after I left the court. I wanted to see what Castro and the others on that camp had to say for themselves face-to-face, still unhappy with attempts to assist the police in removing our camp and attempting to have us arrested, the day we set up the camp.

Predictably, on arrival no one was at camp, so zero resistance to the industry again, and no one there to face me eye-to-eye when a van load of public order police headed towards me. This place was incredibly rural: the police were clearly waiting for me, and those working with the police had hidden, knowing of my imminent arrival. Suddenly, Kirsty appeared, the same individual who had been with Pippa King, the day I checked both sites out with Shaun before deciding which area to place a camp, so she could have been the only person to alert those at Daneshill.

"I never called the police!" she shouted at me.

"I never said you did," I replied.

Kirsty was at Barton Moss and always wore an FBI cap, which I thought was strange at the time, especially as she would have her hands up when police were aggressive, as a sign of no-resistance. I then did more research and found photos of her at an Occupy protest in Paliament square, where just as at Barton Moss, she had her hands up with palms facing out, just before a police raid on a tent that she was outside. It was all too peculiar.

After all that drama, the police just stared at me, in an intimidating manner, as they slowly passed me in their van.

"Well, my bail conditions have been dropped so I'm allowed to be here," my look replied.

The police asked Kirsty if everything was ok, to which she replied: "Yes".

Did the police turn up to protect her in some way?

Soon after, I went to Crawberry Hill to see everyone there, knowing I'd be a lot more welcome. The only other time I actually went to, what I called, Castro's camp after this day, Castro tried to placate me with the offering of tea and cake. But I was having none of it, it felt like she was looking to find a weakness in me or hoping to manipulate me into doing things her way. I don't know why I sensed this, but I did. It might have been because of how other people on camp had fallen in line behind her.

This division in the campaign was not at Barton Moss; something had changed. I was beginning to wonder if some members of the movement were on the payroll of intelligence services and there to thwart the protest. I had read articles over the previous six months about infiltrated movements and undercover agents in various environmental groups over the previous twenty five years, and I was beginning to think this was happening on a much broader scale within this movement. The true story of Britain's secret police is described in a book called *Undercover* by Rob Evans and Paul Lewis. Reading that book left me considering the possibility that serious crimes could be committed by undercover officers, and they could even escape punishment. Although historically that infiltration had been predominantly male, the anti-fracking movement was dominated by females, so I wasn't swayed by the idea of which gender would be used by the state the most.

Consequently, and from what I'd now witnessed, I had my suspicions about certain people, but little clear evidence. Some people may say this was paranoia, but I was well aware of how people's stories and comments were altering, making me wonder what the truth was. At times, it felt like I was being gaslighted. It just made me more vigilant in my words and actions. I always made it clear who I was and what my aims were, these were the foundations I needed going forward. The whole experience narrowed my circles, with my allegiance generally with those with the same resistance ethos as me, with faith in decentralised community protest principles, rather than a connection to any larger organisation.

Crawberry Hill Tower Eviction

On the twenty-ninth of July, the police finally came to evict the tower obstructing the gates at Crawberry Hill. Once the thirty-five days was up, camp was on high alert, so emotions were quite high. For me, these events are just part of the process, so I was prepared to just take everything in my stride. I slept outside in that tower the night before, with George Brown on a pallet bed opposite me, so that I could peacefully resist the eviction. We chatted for some time, him telling me stories of his military days. I wanted to sleep in the tower, so I could resist for as many hours as possible, and this was my second consecutive night. It was a lovely warm night, so I was blessed to be sleeping outside in a beautiful environment.

I woke up again to the birds singing and no police. I could smell the fire burning and the cooking of food. I didn't think for one moment, that eviction was about to take place shortly after, it just felt like another day. That morning, within minutes of me leaving the structure to speak to other camp members and get myself a morning brew, the police and the NET stormed the tower and the surrounding area.

The police stood back and allowed the NET to do the work beyond the heras fence we had constructed in front of the tower. Brown, still inside, had time to scale the structure to grab the Johnny Roger flag and wave it before anyone else. I never thought anything of it, at the time; again, I was always more concerned about stopping fracking. Brown avoided arrest as he voluntarily came down from the structure within minutes and walked up and down the road with the flag in front of the cameras playing out on livestream. The six locals who were arrested were all just exercising their rights to protest on public land outside the fenced-off area. Other locals could not gain access to the protest area as the police had closed all roads leading to the location.

On Brown's climb down I thought, *that's a bit odd. Why would you not stay up there till they forced you down? Enjoy your glory at the top of the tower! Why sleep in the tower, if you were not going to delay proceedings even more?* At this point, I would have been waving the flag at the top for as long as possible. But maybe he had reasons to not be arrested; family, work, I don't know. We all make different decisions. Come to think of it, I didn't really know that much about him. Doubt and suspicion were creeping in: could he have waited for me to vacate the tower, before giving police the call? The timing was uncanny. Once that thought was in my head, I kept wondering who Brown was, or was working for.

The only eviction that took place was the tower, not the camp, which was situated on the verge. So as soon as the police left and the NET was still present but protecting the private land, we began building a tower on the verge to their amazement. Protests were becoming more organised, and more widespread, which was fantastic in terms of fighting fracking. We were proving to be a strong, intelligent and effective community, starting to worry the state enough to brand us domestic extremists. We must have been doing something right.

Ten

Lancashire Nanas, Occupy and Reclaim the Power

THE BARTON MOSS protests had finished two months earlier, so activists and 'actor-vists' who had been at Barton Moss occupied a site in Davyhulme in Manchester. By actor-vist, I mean key players embedded in the movement, presumably by the police, to gather intelligence or steer the protests a certain way. It may sound like paranoid delusion, but events that unfolded were to reveal more of this game-playing by the state. I have no idea why the site in Davyhulme was occupied, unless it was a diversion tactic, because there was no immediate threat there and other active camps could have been chosen to make more impact on the fracking industry. Simultaneously, however, Cuadrilla employed security guards to occupy both their designated fields at Preston New Road (PNR) and Roseacre in Lancashire, with several tents. Was Cuadrilla making sure both sites were unable to be occupied by activists while they were in Davyhulme?

Soon after, in the early hours of the seventh of August, a group called the Lancashire Nanas, including their self-declared 'Queenie', Tina Rothery, occupied the field adjacent to the PNR site. Somewhat strangely, George Brown was also there, which roused my suspicions from the start. From then on, the Lancashire Nanas became prominent activist/actorvists in the wider anti-fracking community. What I did not know at this point was the importance this group name would play, rather than the nanas themselves.

The nanas against fracking movement originates from the Lismore community in New South Wales, Australia. There a group of grandmothers known as the Knitting Nanas Against Gas, participate in non-violent protest against the coal seam gas industry, which is a broadly similar and equally toxic technique to fracking. In 2013, a version of the knitting nanas began in Balcombe, bringing tea, cakes and craftivism to the gates of the Cuadrilla site. Tina Rothery was at Balcombe, so possibly the idea for the Lancashire nanas originated from there. However, I saw no reason why there had to be a group called the Lancashire Nanas, because it could be seen as division from the Knitting Nanas worldwide group, who were already such a force for good. Why would you not use the same name? I thought climate change was a global movement? In Australia, where the brand is the same throughout the country, there are no leaders, but here in England there was Tina Rothery declaring herself 'Queenie'. Why?

What troubled me about this occupation in 2014 was the area size of the Section 6 taken by a dozen Lancashire nanas and Brown – it was massive, about the size of forty football pitches. Normally it's just a small section of a field, as near to the drill site as possible. This occupation was right next to the most high-profile piece of designated land in the country, being protected by security night and day, set up on the adjacent field. If the camp was planning to stay for as long as possible and gather large numbers, I could see the reasoning behind the whole piece of land. But from the outset, this nanas' camp only had ambitions to stay for three weeks and no longer. Something didn't quite add up.

After Rothery had time to do her press rounds following the taking of the field, the nanas were joined the following weekend by RTP, who had chosen this destination for their yearly gathering. In her media appearances, Rothery was once again claiming she was simply a concerned mother and grandmother, only involved with activism because of fracking. However, later it materialised that the key people involved in this occupation had history with various larger climate change organisations and the Occupy movement. Furthermore, she was already involved in social justice movements via the Climate Camp splinter groups and RTP, of which many of its key players were also involved in the Occupy protest at St Paul's Cathedral, in October 2011. I noticed nothing out of the ordinary about Rothery when I met her at Barton Moss, and often to spoke to her in the company of Brown when she turned up. She clearly knew Brown already as would spend most of her time talking to him, but sticking with someone you knew wasn't particularly unusual with a person new to a camp.

This Rothery/RTP camp would be where they'd plan and action a national day of protests, as Climate Camp did before them. It seemed a bit odd they'd picked PNR, because, at the time, Cuadrilla didn't even have planning permission and the West Newton site was active, whereas nothing was likely to be happening at PNR for some time. Many activists, including myself were surprised by the decision to camp there, when they could have had much more significant impact to the fracking industry spending their week disrupting Rathlin Energy's operations instead. But here was this big organisation supporting the nanas' occupation. So was the occupation likely led by Rothery on behalf of unknown others?

There were three key campaigners at RTP at the time, Ewa Jasiewicz, Danielle Paffard and Robbie Gillett. I knew Jasiewicz was a social justice journalist, trade union organiser, who was also involved in the Occupy protests. Paffard had been involved in the climate campaign for many years, was educated at Wadham College, Oxford and is the daughter of Roger Paffard, former executive of High Street chocolatier Thorntons and stationery giant Staples. I thought these campaigners were a force for good when I met them. At the time, I was unaware of Jasiewicz' and Gillett's links to Occupy, Rothery and Brown, but their choice of destination made more sense when I found this out later.

On the one hand, it seemed to make sense for both anti-fracking and climate change groups to join together, after all everyone wanted a greener planet, a healthier future for all. Yet where had they been when we needed more people to hold up the industry at Barton Moss and why were they not in West Newton now? And why the sudden need for leaders in the movement?

The decision of where to go for the RTP summer camp would have appeared to have been made at a meeting of activists at Grow Heathrow. I was not there, but good friends were, and through their knowledge and my own research I was coming to understand how the organisations' decisions were made, according to their experienced 'consensus' and 'cooperation' building techniques. Sounds like a great idea, but, in fact, it is another illusion of democracy, where you vote on something already decided by the leaders. You may be present and think you are participating, but actors/agents spread around the group direct the decision. Hypocritical given that these same people called the current system of politics we live under in the UK 'unjust and undemocratic' in 2011. If genuine activists had been able to properly decide, rather than the actorvists with the historical connection between Climate Camp and Occupy members, Rothery, Brown and Jasiewicz, the RTP summer camp would surely have been at West Newton, where it would have had maximum effect. But why was PNR chosen instead?

I stayed at this RTP camp for a week, as I was not aware of the campaign's hierarchal structure, at the time. I even took part in nationwide actions by the group, allegedly only planned during the week. This process came about by anyone at the camp putting their name forward to take part, which of course I did, fresh from my recent experiences in activism and keen to do more. On one certain day, people were put into groups and met in tents. Our tent was a teepee with about a dozen people in it. We had drawn (allegedly) the IGas headquarters in Mayfair, London, for a direct action, which we had to plan from scratch, including travel, for which there were abundant camp funds. We had Big Dan from Occupy in our group, who had only just a few months back, backed out of our direct action at Barton Moss. He sat through the whole discussions and plans, so he knew every detail about it. However, I was not one bit surprised when he dropped out again on the morning we were setting off for London.

Heading to IGas HQ the next morning, I quickly went on ahead with others on a recce of the area as we got close to the building. It appeared that IGas knew we were coming, and when, because two security guards were outside on the doorstep. *Do they always have security outside their fairly innocuous offices?* I wondered. *Or did they somehow know we were coming?* Undeterred, but a little surprised, we tried to get into the building but the guards shut the door quickly so we had our protest outside instead. We blocked the entrance, waving banners and attracting people's attention for a few hours and took some pictures for media purposes. It would have been more successful if we'd been able to storm the building. I thought, our plans were leaked to Intelligence Services in advance.

There were thirteen actions around the country that day. The most publicised was, of course, Rothery, Daniels, Evans, Samede, Brown and Jasiewicz' action at Cuadrilla's HQ at the time, in Blackpool, where activists and actorvists successfully occupied the building and after several hours managed to somehow leave the building supposedly without the police noticing, and therefore no one was arrested. What was the chance of the most high-profile offices being a successful action, and every other activity apart from one close to our London action, being a failure? The other successful London action even took place outside on scaffolding, rather than inside the building, so one could say that wasn't as successful as intended, either.

It now seemed to me and many others that intelligence had every other action covered but not the number one target, just around the corner from the occupied field, even with Cuadrilla having a twenty-four-hour security service, heavily involving RTP and Occupy leaders. At the time, I never thought it through in great detail because I was still relatively inexperienced but was beginning to become more suspicious with anyone Occupy and RTP related, thanks to Dan's early arrest at Barton Moss and his two last-minute back downs, events at West Newton and this day's actions.

The following day, the camp wrapped up and people set off home, merrily vacating the field we could have held for future use. To this day, this was the only occupation in the anti-fracking movement where activists gave the land back without an eviction. What was going on? Had this occupation been planned in advance, with police, industry and security services, so Cuadrilla security did not have to occupy PNR and Roseacre themselves? It was feasible that it had, so Cuadrilla would have their land secure with an injunction before unmanaged grassroots activists occupied it.

§

Several days after the camp had ended, a 'persons unknown' injunction court hearing took place on Thursday the twenty-eighth of August 2014, at Manchester Civil Justice Centre. Persons unknown injunctions are used, I suspect to deter from naming individuals, because the omission of some would raise suspicion of why leading campaigners are not named, whilst those grassroots activists who use their alienable right to unmanaged protest are named. Surely, Cuadrilla had enough from social media and mainstream media appearances to know certain peoples names. I attended the hearing to find out more. Mr Simon Pook was representing Rothery, who wanted to join the proceedings as the third defendant. Why, I had no idea, because it was inevitable the Judge would grant the injunctions sought for land at PNR and Roseacre. During that hearing, on behalf of Rothery, the Judge stated that:

"Mr. Pook complained that he had had insufficient time to consider and assimilate all of the court documents. I therefore allowed some time before lunch to do so; and after lunch he indicated that, nevertheless, he would be applying for an adjournment because he wished to put in evidence in answer to the claim."

However, there was no opposition to the claimant's entitlement to possession of the land from Rothery's counsel. In fact, Rothery allegedly sought adjournment to, "challenge certain parts of the claimant's evidence as the use, or misuse, to which the occupied land had been put".

Hodge adjourned the hearing until the second of October giving Rothery six weeks to prepare her defence. However, with no opposition to the land injunction, challenging statements was a bizarre decision, because it seemed to be wasting court time.

The Roseacre Wood red herring

Roseacre Wood was another site simultaneously going through the County Council planning process for exploratory drilling and then fracking. The hamlet of Roseacre is several miles away from Preston New Road. However, the chance of Cuadrilla being successful at Roseacre Wood was slim compared to PNR because of its deep rural location. The general feeling I got from the Lancashire campaign was that the lanes around that area were narrow and winding, making it hard for the HGVs to even get to. On a recce of the area later, I too came to that conclusion. I wondered if the Roseacre development might have been a red herring to appear to make the whole planning process look democratic, granting one site planning permission and not the other.

The Chair of the Roseacre Awareness Group (RAG) was a woman called Barbara Richardson. At one of their earlier meetings, a slide promoting fracking elsewhere but not at Roseacre Wood was circulated. These people are generally known as NIMBYs or Not in My Back Yard campaigners who don't mind damage done to other areas, just not theirs. I have nothing against nimbys so long as their participation in the anti-campaign ends there. This annoyed community members at PNR because they interpreted the slides as Roseacre saying PNR was more suitable. An email on the eleventh of September from RAG tried to deny this was the case. Was this why Cuadrilla were protecting land around Roseacre Wood though?

If Barbara Richardson and RAG were for fracking elsewhere, the last thing they would want is anti-fracking protestors occupying a field in their village. Moreover, if they were not opposing fracking everywhere, per se, they would be much more likely to work with Cuadrilla. The ambiguous group name is a giveaway when the vast majority of local groups nationally were titled 'Village/Town/County...Against Fracking', Or 'Frack Free....' not the rather wooly 'Awareness'. It suggested having a 'balanced awareness', of the industry, buzzwords the oil and gas industry PR people used at pro-fracking events in communities. I was surprised to learn someone pro-fracking was positioning herself as a vital member of the Lancashire campaign against it.

§

At the return court date, which I also attended, Rothery had zero evidence, so the court ordered her to pay £55,000 costs. Cuadrilla's lawyers pointed out only case management directions were being sought in relation to the damages claim at the previous hearing. Therefore, the question remained would Cuadrilla have received damages at all? The Judge in his judgement said, "It is wrong to say that the costs of today were not caused by Ms. Rothery because, but for her involvement, the matter would have been put to bed on 28 August."

Another essential factor of this case, which I was also unaware of until a later date, was that Cuadrilla's lawyers appeared to have been given the two year injunction from Rothery's proposals. Mr. Roscoe of Eversheds LLP, working on behalf of Cuadrilla, sought that there should only be a time-limited injunction to expire some twenty-eight days after notification of the planning application's final determination. He addressed the reasons for the injunction's continuation, in his skeleton argument. He then made the point that Rothery had *not* objected to the continuation of the request and indeed accepted, "should continue it for two-years," paraphrasing, "which, as Ms. Rothery's counsel acknowledged, was a period rather longer than Cuadrilla presently proposed."

Why had she offered the industry an injunction longer than they were asking? If she had not become a defendant, Cuadrilla's injunction would not have had the longer timescale. Was Rothery working with Cuadrilla's security to make sure the field had an injunction for as long as possible? The evidential statements she made about future occupations of the land during the camp, certainly looked that way in Cuadrilla's court evidence. For example, "Rothery had appeared on a video saying that if Cuadrilla were to start building works, then the land could be re-invaded, and the campaigners and protestors had every intention of doing so."

I had not understood these issues immediately because I had no experience of legal matters in Civil Courts and like most others, was there to support the anti-fracking campaign, and only interested in the outcome. At this point, we still thought Rothery was part of our movement and were only concerned with whether an injunction would be granted or refused. It was only a couple of years later, when reading court papers fully, that I realised these baffling points, but it's significant enough to raise at this point.

Importantly, now she was a named defendant, so would always be the first to be made aware of any changes to the injunction at PNR. This second point was an important factor, which led to myself and nine-others witnessing first-hand how Rothery was to operate on behalf of Cuadrilla, Lancashire Constabulary and what would become a hierarchical FFL, two years later. Was this why she became a named defendant in the first place?

Eleven

The End of East Yorkshire Campaign

THAT WAS IT for camping for me for a while. I went back to continue my studies, starting modules three and four of my undergraduate degree. Except for a stint over at Crawberry Hill, I rarely left home, which confined me to being a keyboard warrior. That winter stay at Crawberry Hill, during university Christmas break, was by far the coldest I had ever camped in. What had been a beautiful summer enjoying the South Wolds, free from traffic, had now turned to a re-opened road and temperatures close to minus-ten on some nights and not reaching above zero in the day time.

Thankfully by now, a community member had donated a static caravan to the camp, which was on the verge in between structures and tents, so we were able to keep warm with a log burner inside. One morning during this period, we gathered at the gates, as we did daily, which were now manned by eight to ten security guards. Soon after, about forty police officers turned up in vans for just six of us, which I found ridiculous. This location was twelve miles outside Hull, a city presumably with all sorts of crimes being committed, and yet here were Humberside Police, wasting taxpayer's money for the thirty minutes they were there, because there were obsessed with denying us protest at any cost.

Finally, on the three evenings leading up to an organised solidarity day, the Crawberry campaign delivered Humberside Police a blow. A group of about thirty of us managed to successfully slow-walk the security workers' minibus out of the site, even though the police were still trying to enforce zero-tolerance. It was only for about three-hundred metres, but we were delighted. Yet again, it showed that it was numbers on the ground that swayed the balance in our favour over the police and industry. It was also proof that the industry could be stopped at any time by enough people. We had everything in our favour; these protests were taking place at a time of large cuts in police budgets. Everywhere I went now, it was apparent we had to fight peacefully for our rights to protest, which was not easy when every police force was choosing to assault people. On each of those evenings, slow-walking the minibus, the police waded in pushing people off the road into hedges or knocking us to the floor, repeatedly using violence to stop our right to peacefully protest. Where was it all going to lead?

On Sunday the eleventh of January 2015, the solidarity day took place at Crawberry Hill, with a good turnout of people on a cold day with a brisk wind. Community gatherings such as this are one of the most productive events in any campaign because they break down any class or label barriers with everyone coming together for a common cause. More importantly, it brings the national campaign to the drill site, for a day, which means campaigners from all over the country get to meet each other for the first time and see what's going on elsewhere. Local updates, information and skills are shared, which really helps when everyone goes back to their own campaigns to continue with their input, boosted by having made connections with people in similar situations in their areas.

Nine days later, the camp faced eviction. The East Riding of Yorkshire Council claimed the structures we had built on the verge were a danger to other road users and must come down. This was just nonsense; we had been there for six months since the previous tower eviction, without one incident involving the traffic on this rural B road. But the law didn't like the tower because it meant we could see police or industry coming, long before they could catch the camp by surprise. In the weeks leading up to that eviction, we had one certain police officer, who would never speak to anyone including locals, driving past regularly, checking camp out. I thought he might be ex-military checking out what was needed for eviction and how it could be done, in a minimal timescale.

There were only about eight on base the morning of the eviction, including the retired Brown, all of a sudden, who claimed he had just cycled the twelve miles from Hull, up hill, in the dark, and on icy roads in sub-zero weather, with the biting wind in his face the whole way. As usual, we had been outside the compound gates from seven o'clock waiting in the hard frost for the morning security switch over. But that morning there was no shift change, and by about eight-fifteen we were all frozen to the bone. We decided to go and warm ourselves in the caravan, make a brew and discuss the unusual circumstance.

A few minutes later, someone opened the door, and a convoy of police vans, with dozens of police, were coming through the camp. It was as if they had been alerted that we were all in the caravan and the time was right to strike. I ran out and tried to dive into the road with a lock-on tube. Sadly, Welsh Dan and I didn't have time to connect ourselves together, and the officers dragged us both roughly on to the verge, before arresting us. Had the lock-on been successful, we would have both been there for hours while the police cutting team got us out. In that weather, we might have been frozen solid: but if that's what it took, we were prepared to do it. Over a half-mile stretch or more of the road was now closed off to anyone but police.

For their operation command post that morning, the police were using a large, stable complex, one and a half miles away on the same road. They took me and Dan there to decide what they would do with us. We were held there for half an hour and watched out the window as an all-in-one gazebo was being stretched out, and tables being place under it. It felt like we were being held at a military interrogation base. During our stay there, we watched as a convoy of eviction equipment passed on the road outside, heading towards the camp, including JCBs and other camp dismantling equipment. We never actually left the van and were taken to a Clough Road police station in Hull. So that was another arrest, my fourth unlawful one, the charges being dropped this time because we had video evidence of the police dragging me across the road. With the eviction came the end of the Crawberry Hill Protection Camp. When I looked back on that day, and remembered the previous tower eviction with the flag-waving, I began questioning Brown's involvement much more.

Following this final eviction, the local activists took over, organising a rota so that most days there would be a small group of the 'geriactivists' standing in rain, snow or frost, monitoring the site and registering continued local opposition to fracking. In the summer months they also organized 'pop-ups' on local commuter roads in the evenings to maintain their peaceful protest. Rathlin finally gave up in August 2015 – a victory for the combined power of the protection camp and locally organised activists. The site is now a free-range chicken farm.

During my time in East Yorkshire, I spoke at public meetings in Walkington, Beverley, Holderness and Skirlaugh. Standing up in front of a hall full of people was not something I was natural at to begin with, but I got better and more confident as time went on. It had to be done to encourage the locals to join us in the fight against fracking. Still, my personal development had come a long way in eighteen months. At the time of writing in 2021, the West Newton campaign is still active, a downside of stakeholder participation in a landowner dominated location.

Twelve

Politics and Positioning of Players

IN 2015, A General Election was held in the UK, and I hoped for a change of government, ideally towards the Labour Party as I thought they would put a stop to fracking. At the time, Labour were still sitting on the fence about the matter, but there seemed more chance of lobbying them with success, rather than ever hoping to get the Conservatives to change tack. I had long been a Labour voter, but their lack of opposition to austerity policies had infuriated me, and the Green Party of England and Wales better represented my views on conserving the environment. So, I had previously given the Green Party my vote. However, my support for them was in the balance this time, when I and others began to question a particular Green Party member's personal motives.

Tina Rothery, Brown's close friend, had become the first ever Green Party candidate for the constituency of Tatton in Cheshire. The parliamentary seat of Tatton was the seat of the former Chancellor George Osbourne. Of course, many activists at the time believed it was just a publicity stunt because she had zero chance of winning. However, the anti-fracking movement was diverse in its political affiliations, so it concerned me that a Green Party candidate, a self-proclaimed leader of anti-fracking, would even stand for one particular party, especially as she claimed the system needed dismantling. Was she using the anti-fracking movement for her political gain? Or using the opportunity to further her self-proclaimed leader status within the campaign? Probably a combination of both, and all options were dangerous, in my opinion, because no one knew her background before Occupy. She could have been police, intelligence services or industry, for all we knew. The last thing the movement needed was for it to be centralised around this one person.

§

A month later, on the twenty-ninth of June 2015 Lancashire County Council's long-awaited decision on the application to frack the Preston New Road (PNR) site, was announced. In extraordinary circumstances, that we never expected, the government's hope for a shale gas revolution suffered its first significant defeat. Lancashire Councillors decided to reject Cuadrilla's plans and in doing so, defied their legal and planning advisor's guidance to grant Cuadrilla permission for their proposed site at PNR. This refusal was due to concerns over an "unacceptable noise impact", and the "adverse urbanising effect on the landscape".

Boy, did we celebrate! But we knew it was inevitable that Cuadrilla would appeal this shock decision, especially as it was seen by many as a 'test case' for how other local councillors would react to similar proposals around the country. Although we were overjoyed at this significant setback for the industry, campaigners knew the fight was far from over. Nevertheless, it was a celebration time for everyone but Cuadrilla and the government.

Tina Rothery, was outside the council talking to the media and leading the celebration. She appeared to be taking all the credit when she had not even entered the council buildings to object. Had she single-handedly fought Cuadrilla's proposals? Not at all, many others in Lancashire had worked hard on the ground in the campaign. But with that media bias rearing its head again, Rothery was starting to be the established spokesperson in the Lancashire campaign that the mainstream media would talk to. Despite claiming she was a novice campaigner, just a concerned grandmother compelled to fight fracking, much of her chat was now about climate change.

In September, the Lancashire Nanas headed to Oxford to the home of David Cameron with Vivienne Westwood in a Talk Fracking sponsored tank. Great publicity I thought, anything Vivienne Westwood was involved in always brought media attention. Westwood and her son Joe Corre's peripheral participation became more evident at this time, with their central message aimed at combatting climate change. Unfortunately, the tank was spewing pollution all over the countryside on the way to Cameron's house. Some of the nanas in Lancashire recorded this but Rothery made sure none of them released the footage. With funding from Lush (the cosmetics company that had a social justice pot for many campaign groups) and Corre, Rothery and this group of nanas started travelling around the country, apparently jubilant at stopping fracking, although it had not been stopped. Whichever group they went to, they'd give a Nana bib to someone, strategically choosing people from each area to join their ranks, even if they were not a grandmother. Of course, this had the effect of centralising local community campaigns at the hands of Rothery, who would then be able to know what all the central campaigners in each area were up to. Simultaneously to the Lancashire Nanas, Rothery also created a sister group called Nanashire for just that. The different groups also provided increased opportunities for putting call-outs for funds. Sometimes Rothery asked for donations directly in her own name, other times the call would go something like 'nanas can't fight fracking with cake alone, please donate.......' Diverting grassroots funding? or a signal for climate change backed private funding?

People who obtained a Nanashire bib were blithely unaware of this; from the outside, the Nanas looked like a great idea and probably had the effect of bringing people into the movement. But all I and others could see was one person getting all the praise, while using others to further her leadership and centralisation of the movement. We became very alarmed by this behaviour. So, I shared my strong belief publicly that a centralised campaign would be the movement's downfall. When a campaign against a local concern happens naturally in a grassroots movement, it's usually non-hierarchical and people from all walks of life rise to the challenge of protecting their community. They become knowledgeable about the issue, eloquent at speaking about it and militant in their opposition to it. Just as I'd done. Most importantly, grassroots anti-fracking campaigning and protesting was appearing to work, with the onshore oil and gas industry backing away from many long-held sites, once vocal opposition galvanised communities.

§

Vivienne Westwood and Joe Corre had visited Upton in November, where Vivienne D-locked herself around the neck to a post, as a statement of the only option people had left against the fracking industry. The end of 2015, saw the barricades well and truly fortified and campaigners came from all over the country, to build and hold the fort. The start of 2016, began with a call-out for more people, so I stayed there for the weekend. Rothery and several of her nanas turned up, too. The atmosphere was frosty between us all, but I just stayed alert to resist any eviction attempt.

However, while I was back at home studying, the eviction took place on the morning of the twelfth of January. Nine people were arrested, two men for obstructing police and another for obstructing highway. A man and woman were arrested for obstructing a High Court officer, a man for failing to comply with a Section thirty-five notice, and another for police assault and aggravated trespass. I was gutted I wasn't there, but it would probably have led to yet another arrest for me. Successfully, no drilling ever took place at Upton, with IGas pulling out of the proceedings, via a statement the following month. That night we celebrated with the local community over a few drinks.

Thirteen

North Yorkshire Campaign

DURING THE CAMPAIGN to prevent Third Energy from fracking at Kirby Misperton, North Yorkshire, Frack Free Ryedale set up many separate groups to tackle various aspects of strategy. One of those grassroots campaigners, Sue Gough had been at an earlier meeting in Huddersfield, when we emphasised the importance of decentralised campaigning. That meeting was called for, because at the time the experienced engineer Mike Hill was pro-regulation (he believed the industry could be stopped by regulations). Geza Frackman was a close friend of Hill's, so we were preventing this pro-regulation trajectory gaining a foothold in other communities. The evidence from around the world showed once the industry had a foothold, it would be more difficult to stop. As I knew all wells failed eventually, I was determined for nowhere to be fracked. Lead campaigners from across the North West attended. Rothery was the only key person who chose not to attend that meeting.

The Yorkshire Nanas were created very early on, Sue Gough being one of them. This group of kind, concerned, genuine elders, like the majority of those in Lancashire had created their own personalised blue bibs with the emblem of the Yorkshire white rose on, thus keeping the movement from being centralised and doing things their way. The group was strong and diverse; people joined in actions and rallies when they could, taking a bib to wear on coach journeys or at venues. The work they did was varied, always good-humoured and peaceful, often including knitting or crochet, and always including cake.

The jubilant scenes that surrounded the Lancashire success the previous year, turned to disappointment for the national campaign on the twenty-third of May 2016, when fracking received the go-ahead in North Yorkshire, in one of the most beautiful parts of the British countryside. This County Council judgement was a landmark decision paving the way for drilling in rural areas across England. The fracking operation by Third Energy in Kirby Misperton, near Malton, would now beat Cuadrilla to be the first frack in Britain in five years. If those tests showed that shale gas could be extracted successfully, full-scale production would begin later. The planning authority received more than 4,000 objections, mainly on environmental grounds, with only thirty-two letters supporting the application. But permission was granted. It was a bitter blow to all of us, especially as energy analysts had just warned that industry investors were losing interest in the fledgling shale gas industry.

For two days (Thursday and Friday), campaigners including myself, from Northern England had joined North Yorkshire residents in a gathering of support outside the North Allerton council building. The lovely Yorkshire nanas were out in force, with plenty of tea and cake, and a constant supportive presence on the lawns outside the council building. Inside, in front of eleven council officers, members of the public raised their objections, which we could hear on the loudspeaker outside. Residents covered everything from environmental harm, increased traffic on rural roads, plus air and light pollution to the effects on health and potential to damage homes. That council decision was announced on the Monday after, no doubt knowing many people had only made plans to protest for only those two days the end of the previous week.

Although I was not involved in the occupation of the land that would be central to fracking resistance at Kirby Misperton, I watched on gleefully as it was born soon after that council decision. However, not long after, a tractor belonging to the landowner with cultivating blades on the back, drove on to the field and started ripping the turf up, leaving a five-metre line across the area. In the drama, Lou Hammond was thrown to the floor by a worker connected to the landowner, which enabled an agreement shortly after to be made for camp to stay.

A lad called Eddie Thornton, the son of a local GP became the face of this camp, living there for the duration. He became the camp spokesperson in the media and made sure the press (even the BBC) had a good press relationship with the camp. Liaising well between camp and community, he inspired other local residents to get involved and feel safe to join in the protests. Direct action in resistance to Third Energy was the cornerstone of what he wanted to create, in which he would later play a pivotal role.

A few weeks later, on a break from studies, I headed over to Kirby Misperton from Liverpool to build what was now my fourth camp kitchen, the finest one I had created. The experience in building the others had the design perfected to match the army tarp, which covered it. The kitchen was some ten-metres long and five-metres wide, with a door and windows, and pallets on the floor covered in plywood. The frame was built using some five-by-two timber for roof joists and pallets for the walls, covered by the tarp. There was a cooking area, shelving for produce and a food service area that opened out at one end of structure. Outside there was a washing up area with an aluminum sink, and a drainpipe from the roof to recycle the rainwater. The camp cooked here but also had meals brought by various locals. One of whom, Derek, I never always saw eye-to-eye with. He was a lovely gentleman but wanted to work with the police, which I still classed as working with the industry. My experience had shown me there was no point negotiating with police or the industry. One would expect consensus and cooperation from councillors, but this wasn't just a minor council issue, this was the start of the industrialisation of the countryside.

Fourteen

Rothery vs Cuadrilla - or Political Pantomime?

BACK IN LANCASHIRE, on the sixth of October, locals were devastated when the then Communities Secretary Sajid Javid decided upon the Lancashire appeals to start fracking in their area too, with one decision in favour of Cuadrilla starting work at PNR. PNRAG, which consisted of about ten locals, led by chair Pat Davies, put up a sterling fight against Cuadrilla's appeal which heard evidence over a period of weeks. Interestingly, not one NGO supported PNRAG despite being asked to help this small grassroots group up against Cuadrilla, who were openly declaring their plans to make their site outside the populated village of Little Plumpton, 'the largest fracking sight in Europe.' The decision was a huge blow for local democracy. Why would all environmental NGOs not support a community threatened with the largest fracking site in Europe? Had these NGOs been involved in consensus and cooperation meetings with Cuadrilla?

Javid kicked the Roseacre can down the road and couldn't make a decision one way or the other. He gave Cuadrilla the opportunity to present further evidence as to how they could mitigate concerns around traffic management. On the face of it Roseacre wasn't out of the woods. However, this could have been the carrot for the somewhat pro-fracking group RAG to toe the line and sabotage as much as possible any opposition to PNR. After the site at PNR had been built and drilling well under way, the decision was finally announced that planning would not be granted at Roseacre. This second decision further verified my suspicion that the government and the industry were using the whole process to give the illusion of democracy on planning decisions. Later it would appear that the so-called success of Roseacre not being drilled, gave Richardson and Roberts a foot in the door of other communities to try and lay the foundations for negotiations with the police on how we would be allowed to protest elsewhere.

In December 2016, Tina Rothery was finally back in court to face Cuadrilla for the non-payment of the £55,000 fine she had received over two years earlier, in the 2014 PNR and Roseacre land injunction case. In all the years of the anti-fracking campaign, this was the biggest media circus I have ever seen for an individual, and only third to the publicity surrounding Lancashire County Council and North Yorkshire decisions themselves. The media and mainstream NGOs were awash with the phrase 'Grandmother faces jail', a classic 'emotionally attached' form of manipulation. Not to mention the social media hysteria around the hashtag #IAMTINATOO masterminded by Rothery's team, the Machiavellian Brown and Claire Stephenson (soon to be promoted to FFL's media team, after causing strife within the PNRAG Group). Stephenson was heard boasting to a friend that she had been recruited by FFL and offered a paid position by the group. If this is true then she was being paid out of funds donated to stop fracking in Lancashire whilst answerable to the chair of FFL, Ian Roberts.

It may have seemed like it was good for everyone to support Tina in court, but something was not right, and many of us were now seriously concerned with Rothery and the actions of certain people in FFL. The campaign nationally was seen as non-hierarchical, but it was quite evident at this point that this group believed they were in charge. Vital members of this hierarchical group, were Rothery and her sister Julie Daniels, Maureen Mills (Halsall), Ian Roberts (RAFF) Barbara Richardson (RAG), Nick Danby, John Hobson (Refraction) and Claire Stephenson.

However, it was only Rothery, Cuadrilla and the Judge who knew what occurred in the court that morning, as no one else was allowed in to observe. Fifteen people were allowed in the court building, including Daniels and Stephenson, and Sue Marshall was also asked to be one of them, when Daniels came outside and grabbed her, most likely to keep her on side. Rothery went into the court room and she told those outside, waiting in corridor, that she had asked for Ruth Hayhurst, the Drill or Drop journalist, to be allowed in as her Mackenzie friend. She said the judge refused Hayhurst on the grounds that she wasn't impartial enough. That didn't make sense as Mackenzie friends aren't meant to be impartial, they are there as your support. She said that 'they' had suggested Ian Roberts. Now why or how would the judge or Cuadrilla suggest Ian Roberts? Why or how would they even know who he was? Roberts was being a steward to the crowd outside, so in the end it appeared that she took Buckley in with her, but it materialised that even she wasn't allowed in the discussion room in the end. Of course, Rothery never went to jail that day, and it is improbable she will ever have to pay the £55,000 to Cuadrilla. So, what was it all about?

On that morning of Rothery's case, Ian Roberts marshalled the protest to the court from Preston Centre. After doing some research on him, I learned that he was the brother of Mark Roberts, the regional lead on public order policing, who had been policing the protests at Barton Moss and was now the leading police officer on anti-fracking protests in Northern England. What a coincidence!

We soon learned that Rothery's sister Julie Daniels was very close pals with Ian Roberts, so we knew it would have been impossible for Brown and Rothery not to know of the Roberts brothers' connection, on her weekly visits to Barton Moss. We also learned from Lancashire campaigners outside the hierarchy showing us a local newspaper article and a BBC online report, that an anonymous person had left over £20,000 on Ian's doorstep in a paper bag in Lytham St Annes in 2012. Ian is reported in the local newspaper as saying he felt certain who ever had left the cash on his door step had intended it for development of a local park. We knew the industry had a history of giving community incentives to get their foot in the door, so was that what this was?

Since 2012, Ian Roberts had been Chair of RAFF and had now become a key member of FFL. Around the time of the £20,000 doorstep incident, he was quoted as saying in regards to resistance to Cuadrilla in Lancashire, "We are not going to chain ourselves to railings or climb the rigging and demand they go away. We will be sensible and grown-up about our protest, but that doesn't mean we are any less steely or that we will be a push-over."

Was he suggesting that those of us taking direct action were not grown-ups? That to be one you had to negotiate with the industry to make sure life was easier for the frackers, also helping ease his brother Mark's policing job? It seemed as if the psychological foundations were being set for a new norm in managed protest. But we were having none of it.

Three weeks after the Rothery media circus and the strange outcome of her case, Cuadrilla started operations at Preston New Road. With no injunction now in place stopping us occupying any land near the site, the much-awaited protests were underway. Although, I was not present because of studies, I watched daily livestreams direct from outside the site entrance.

Before the Ryedale fracking decision was announced, everyone in the movement had long expected that PNR would be the first site of a significant fracture of the rock below the ground, since the earlier moratorium had been lifted. Whether it would be the first or second frack in the UK, it needed stopping. The threat to the environment from earthquakes and well failure was overwhelming by now, which meant the threat of water pollution. The state of Oklahoma in the US had experienced some 585 earthquakes from fracking measuring over three on the Richter scale in 2015 alone, with one measuring over five. Another fracking earthquake that year came in August in British Columbia, when a site operated by Progress Energy Canada, recorded 4.6. The risks remained too great to sit back and allow a gentile, managed protest to take place.

However, activists were unaware of a 'covenant' struck earlier between those who were now at the top of the FFL campaign,

Cuadrilla and Lancashire Constabulary. It wasn't until about five days into the construction of the site at Little Plumpton when Rothery, from the side of a lorry, made people aware that she would oversee the operation and allow only thirteen people to slow-walk lorries behind a fence, for just fifteen minutes at a time. Otherwise, Lancashire Constabulary would enforce a S14 on the whole protest, just as police had in Balcombe. Of course, Cuadrilla had scheduled these fifteen-minute hold-ups into their days after the first day of this managed protest. Anyone likely to break the agreement and obstruct Cuadrilla would not be allowed to participate, which meant the majority of the activist community were basically cut-off from protesting.

Rothery, Daniels and Danby would oversee managing these strategic tactics, on the road behind heras fencing, near the site entrance. It soon came to light there had been a meeting weeks earlier at a nearby cafe, not long after the Rothery court case, where local people in attendance were told not to speak to national activists (meaning those from other areas who went to many different sites) when they came to protest. Roberts even suggested people wore badges so that local (good) protesters could be distinguished from non-local (bad) protestors. Of course, this would establish who Lancashire constabulary would victimise and who they would leave alone, in their anti-fracking policing operation called Manilla. Were these the same Barton Moss tactics used by the same Silver Commander flowing through the hierarchy of the FFL campaign group? Certainly. After all, Mark Roberts was the regional lead on public order policing.

We should have prepared for something like this, but no one would have believed that anyone could tell local and national campaigners how to protest on such a contentious issue as fracking. Or that a lead campaigner in Lancashire was the brother of the regional lead on public order policing in the North West. For the second time in the campaign, we had a small group of people negotiating on behalf of the whole country, how we could protest against the fracking industry, which we had been resisting in the same effective way for years. And their way appeared to be allowing the industry to do what it wanted, with very minor hold-ups, just as Ian Roberts had stated would happen, back in 2012.

These operational negotiations were the confirmation we needed that Rothery and others were working with industry and police directly after many months of suspicions. Why would you do that, when you represented the Green Party, who were claiming we're in a 'climate emergency' and we must act now? They were also the early strands in the attempt to deny the right to protest for everyone. As it was, statistics now showed that around only one in five people supported a UK shale gas industry, so doing a deal to facilitate oil and gas companies angered many long-time campaigners. We saw protest as not only essential, here and now, but also lawful and central to a functioning democracy. Furthermore, local democracy had been working to effectively stop the oil and gas industry getting a foothold in their areas, only to be overturned by the national government. This overriding of local government decisions would be the start of a slippery slope for other communities if they never took an active stand against the industry now.

People's right to protest should always be allowed for, and not on Cuadrilla's and Lancashire Constabulary terms. History has shown us that many of the freedoms we now have were won through protest, not 'consensus and cooperation.' As individuals we have the freedom and the right to protest in any way we chose. It was not up to a small number of people to dictate how everyone protested, no matter what policing the protest cost the taxpayer. How things had changed, since the Suffragette women were given the vote one-hundred-years earlier, won by unmanaged protest. The cost to future generations of a long-term fracking industry far outweighed the immediate costs of any police operation. In any case, these campaigners were forever shouting about protecting future generations from climate change... Or was that just a front too, because they weren't exactly reacting in accordance to their emergency discourse? Could it be that Mark Roberts was working through Ian Roberts, who was working through the sisters Rothery and Daniels on behalf of Lancashire Constabulary who would allow Cuadrilla's operations to go ahead unhindered by protest?

During these early days of the PNR construction, in January 2017, Rothery gave her account of the daily proceedings in a blog each evening. The blog was called 'In the Cuadrilla house', which was a strange title and upset many local people because this was their environment, not Cuadrilla's; I felt their pain and confusion. Furthermore, it sounds similar to the Big Brother house, were people are constantly spied on. One week into site construction, Rothery actually announced her protest deal on her blog for everyone to see, telling the world, she had made an agreement for a fifteen minute slow-walk, with only thirteen people at any given time, because it was the safest way to protest. After a huge backlash from local community members, she then removed the piece and denied she'd ever written it. This lying angered people even more because she was blatantly refuting something she had shared herself on her global platform, that many of us had seen with our own eyes, whilst her team went on a mission to tarnish good people's names for highlighting this fact. People who had long seen Rothery as a beacon of grassroots resistance, now watched on, as the veil slipped.

This behaviour, a technique called 'gaslighting', was being used in the campaign, particularly on social media, on a truly incredible scale. Now, people were questioning what they'd seen, all they knew to be true and even their own sanity. In contrast, those on the peripherals to all this would have bought the dominant narrative of Rothery as a fierce grandmother, a novice campaigner, doing everything she could to stand up to the industry. But this was seeming more and more like a charade. The question on many campaigners mind at the time, was whether Rothery had always been working against us, or was it just a severe case of narcissism. Or did she do a deal with Cuadrilla in court, to work off her £55,000? This was unlikely, because she knew she could easily crowdfund the money before the case.

If this controlled protest had been allowed to happen daily, without activist opposition, you may have needed to book your fifteen-minute slow walk protest a week in advance or face arrest for any other meaningful opposition. Local campaigners and members of PNRAG, Sue Marshall and her son Morgan, were refused entry one morning into what was being called a protest pen. When Sue asked why, she was told, "It was because Morgan had taken photographs the previous time, they had been in." According to Sue, then, "began a brilliant game (from the industry's perspective) of divide and rule. There were the 'good' protestors pitted against the not so good. It didn't take much to get put on the naughty list. Just refuse to be told who you could and couldn't speak to, or ask a question and not follow blindly."

Such differing opinions of what Rothery was about created a huge divide in what had long been a united movement, except for differences between camps in East Yorkshire. It was a sad time for everyone because it divided friends who had met along the way, especially those who lived in other areas of the UK. Many people did not know who to believe; some certainly could not think this grandmother, who the mainstream press and mainstream NGOs had been 'greenwashing' us with, just a couple of months earlier, could be the person myself, locals and other long-time campaigners were witnessing being manipulative and combative daily.

The Barton Moss protests were far less psychologically damaging than this. But what I was witnessing now was miniscule compared to what came after, and what community members had to endure in the times ahead. The good that came from it all was that we realised we could only continue to campaign with those we could trust, those who we had met face-to-face before and knew to be genuine, and those who publicly denounced the covenant.

Meanwhile, the drill site was being built rapidly, with little to no disruption. Something had to change; we had not seen this national control before, so other Lancashire residents including the Marshalls and Bob Dennett asked the wider activist community for support, because they were not prepared to wait for orders from Rothery et al. In normal circumstances, I would have refused because I saw it as a decentralised local issue, but it was clear a small number of people were acting in a centralised manner and it wasn't having an effect on the industry, neither did their tactics represent everyone.

Thankfully, I had now finished my undergraduate study, with a lower second class degree, and I was free to be more active again on the front line. I was certainly not prepared to be denied my rights to protest against the fracking industry. Plus, I had long promised myself that I would sacrifice one day of my life to protect the environment from the industry for the good people of Lancashire ever since I realised the village of Little Plumpton was going to host the first full fracking site, years earlier.

Surely, if everyone in Lancashire who was against fracking blocked the site's entrance for one day, there could be no industry for that day, and then another day, and another, potentially. That's how people had stopped it in parts of Australia, with sheer numbers getting in the way of the operation. It is not 'mob rule'; it is democracy in action, where communities have a say in their communities' future, when local democracy fails. The new infiltrated hierarchy of FFL did not speak for everybody; they just represented a few wealthy people and themselves, very much similar to a citizen's assembly which doesn't allow for full, authentic deliberation of issues, but was steered towards a certain outcome. It was clear others in the community needed to step in to try and stop this toxic industry being allowed to do what it wanted, by people who called themselves the opposition.

How the lorries entered Barton Moss Road

The lorries heading through Barton Moss Camp

On the Frontline at Barton Moss

The IGas drilling site at Barton Moss

Fargo McCann

Yellowbelly

Greater Manchester Police search the Barton Moss anti-fracking camp

Another damp and cold morning on Barton Moss Road

The gathering on camp after Solidarity Sunday

Surfers take to the lorries at Barton Moss in response to Cameron's announcement

Eighty-two-year-old Anne Power sending the TAU on their way

Radioactive substances make their way through camp to IGas site

Police obfuscation in broad daylight

Shale Gas World Conference in Brussels '-All wells fail eventually'

First direct action with lock-on devices at Barton Moss

Arrested after direct action at Barton Moss

How we left Barton Moss Road after protests

Humberside Police officer and his neighbour selling up quick

The Upton Protection Camp near Chester is born

Locals Jon and Val Mager before their arrest at Crawberry Hill

Released from Clough Road Police Station, after our unlawful arrests.

Building the barricades at Crawberry Hill

One tower removed, in defiance another one built

One of Tina Rothery's weekly visits to see George Brown at Barton Moss

The Successful Crawberry Hill Resistance team including the geriactivists

First direct action arrest with footpath protection team

The night we celebrated in Upton when IGas gave up in the North West of England

Fifteen

Activists Begin the Fight Back

THE LAST WEEKEND of that crazy first month at Little Plumpton, which shook the campaign, I went over to the Kirby Misperton Protection Camp for the weekend to catch up with camp members and locals I knew I could trust. The stunning Ryedale countryside was always great for my mental well-being, so I visited as often as my studies would allow. From the moment I arrived in Ryedale, I felt a warm, welcoming embrace of the landscape. I had no intention of planning any actions, just resting for a few days listening to the wildlife - but a few drinks late on the Saturday night changed that.

The thrill of talking about my previous direct action years earlier at Barton Moss, had Eddie Thornton and Louise Hammond excited. Eddie was playing a pivotal role in the Kirby Misperton campaign and saw the chance to show solidarity with Lancashire. Of course, he was hoping Lancashire activists would return the same solidarity when the fracking trucks pulled into North Yorkshire. Eddie was nudging away at me to organise a direct action for PNR, and Louise wanted to take direct action in my company. I was sold on the idea, especially as we would be striking back at Rothery et al, on behalf of the local community and disillusioned campaigners. Furthermore, it would begin an attempt to take back individual power and control in the campaign, rather than the centralised methods being forced on everyone.

My previous experience of direct action, since late 2013, had shown me that once anyone starts it, others follow suit. So that Sunday, we went to the building suppliers and bought the materials needed using camp funds donated by locals. We generally just used plastic pipes with harmless materials wrapped underneath the thick tape to make devices look bulky, so the police cutting team would have to take their time carefully removing them from our arms.

Just as with the t-shirt messages at Barton Moss, the protest was symbolic, so we wrote messages on each device. The central one was addressed to Francis Egan, CEO of Cuadrilla UK, which said 'from the UK Protection Community', as a statement that we were now back in control. Another device, said 'Water is Life' and the third 'The Day Democracy Died', which highlighted the community's overrule by the Secretary of State. In reality, it was this day democracy was reborn, because only this kind of democracy remained.

Setting off early the day of the action, we stopped at a car park at six-thirty, about five minutes from the site, to do a trial run of our exit from vehicles. Suddenly, we saw a convoy of aggregate lorries heading for the site – we knew because of the time and the name on the side - as a car came into the empty car park and attempted to park in between us, to block us off. How did they know our plans? Likely from the Automatic Number Plate Recogition (ANPR) cameras once we arrived in the area.

Anyway, we avoided the car and continued as planned, but the lorries were already inside the site on our arrival, breaking the traffic management plan in the process, which was set for vehicles to go in no earlier than seven o' clock. Nevertheless, Eddie, Louise, Jared Dunne and myself (PNR4), dived out the cars, set ourselves up across the entrance and took action anyway; now nothing else could come in or out. We were positioned legally on public land at the edge of the road and site entrance. Cuadrilla had stolen public land for the entrance, otherwise we would have been situated in the access area, which would have been originally the grass verge and off the road completely. This area of public land was reclaimed a couple of months later, when Louise Boyle a local campaigner consistently highlighted the issue, during her long resistance to Cuadrilla at PNR.

Locked into a tube device with both arms attached to Eddie and Lou next to me across the entrance, I had no intention of ending the protest in an hour, which is what the S14 command required. It was a miserable day and it rained nonstop, but we were left alone by police until lunchtime when their specialist team came to cut us out. Locals gathered in support and Geza Frackman insisted they donate their umbrellas to show appreciation and offer some protection to us lying on the floor in the pissing rain. The protest was very peaceful, even the security in front of the gates were pleasant with us, trying to keep us dry by replacing tarps over us when the wind blew them off. We had our usual team of legal observers keeping an eye on the police, and Ian Crane filmed the events for the wider anti-fracking movement. Once we were cut out, one-by-one, we were arrested and taken to Blackpool Police Station.

The majority of local people were delighted with the action, but it appeared that Rothery and Daniels were not. Online they tried to show they supported us but they stayed on the other side of the carriageway for most of the action and local protestors were confused by her 'having a face like thunder'. It didn't seem to make sense to anyone serious about stopping the progression of the site; apart from a brief moment when Rothery came over to dismiss claims again that she had done a deal, which was still the talk of the town. Neither of them thanked us in person for taking action in Lancashire, which they were claiming to represent in the fight against the industry. Strangely, Daniels was even caught on camera telling the police, "You cannot arrest them!" We weren't sure what that meant, other than it messed with operational plans in some way.

We spent the rest of the day at the police station before being released after midnight, with bail conditions stopping us going back to the site. Thankfully, Ian had booked rooms at a B&B close by, so we didn't have far to go to sleep after a long and exhausting day. We may have been simply lying on th edge of the road for nine hours but the tedium and cold wet weather drained all energy from me.

As expected, following this, many others took similar direct action in the proceeding weeks, even creating a leaderboard for the longest lock-on, which grew from our nine hours to some of around twenty hours. It was great to see many other activists and the wider community slowing down Cuadrilla's operations in this way.

As I had at Barton Moss and Crawberry Hill, I applied to the courts straight away to have my bail conditions removed so that I could go back to the drill site. Strangely, no other arrests after ours faced geographical bail conditions from PNR, they received just bail to appear in court weeks later. I soon realised that agents must be involved in actions that followed, and the authorities required their presence on the road to steer the protests a certain way.

As soon as my bail conditions were dropped at the court hearing in Blackpool, I headed straight back to the drilling site gates with my old friend Bob the Builder from the early days at Barton Moss. On the other side of the road to the entrance, there was Rothery talking to Logic Al. Neither one of them crossed the dual carriageway all the time I was there that day. Rothery thought about approaching, but turned around halfway across the road and went back. Logic Al stayed as far away from me as he could, which was odd because he had been outside the gate during my lock on, when my arms were in a tube. To me, it felt as if both were afraid to come anywhere near me for fear of me asking tough questions in front of the locals they were deceiving. I could have questioned them, but decided that keeping them in suspense of me approaching them, would be just as rewarding.

Months later, in court alongside my co-arrestees Eddie, Jared and Louise, we were found guilty of obstruction of the highway, unlike others who had taken identical direct action after ours. Strangely, our case was deemed to be in the public interest, but some of the others that followed were not. This means that the CPS look at all the evidence and decide whether it's worth going ahead with criminal proceedings or not. There are two limbs to the Code for Crown Prosecutors: the evidential stage and the public interest stage. The first limb has to have a fifty percent chance of success in court and the second involves a much longer list of criteria, but in these cases it's the effect on the local community, of which Cuadrilla is classed as being part of.

Anyway, it was obvious some cases were being treated differently by Lancashire's CPS, as well as the police too. Corruption appeared to be running deep, and from this point it increased steeply and dangerously, in an attempt to destroy all unmanaged protest completely.

The Camp of New Hope

In late February 2017, activists formed a new protest camp near the Little Plumpton site called New Hope. This new base camp sent a defiant statement to the campaign, which Rothery and others were dismantling. However, this renewed positivity would not last long, because by now Little Plumpton was awash with agents and informants, all working together. It was like a virus sweeping through every part of the solidarity within the movement, built over the previous years. Of course, we had been organising for years, so it would have been foolish not to think the authorities were not doing the same. Frackman and Hill had now both realised the pro-regulation argument was redundant, because the safety breaches were already stacking up on site, without much punishment from planning regulators, and the drill site wasn't even built, just the access road.

After those weeks of effective direct actions and now a new camp for activists, the police and industry were keen to take back control. Cuadrilla CEO Francis Egan was telling the world, especially investors, that activists were not slowing down operations. But it was evident to everyone involved that we were; in fact, campaigners who were resisting the industry were well on top. Of course, Rothery and her crew weren't in control of proceedings. So, it was no surprise when soon after that first month of actions, she called out, on social media, for her colleagues in RTP and Occupy to come to Blackpool that coming Saturday. She had the brass cheek to ask for unity when she was anything but for unity, unless she could give the orders.

The NGOs came and planned to occupy the field next to the drilling site, which in earlier circumstances, we would have agreed with and taken an active role. However, if Rothery was organising it, it must have been pre-arranged with the police and Cuadrilla. This NGO involvement was a worrying development, as I'd now counted four or five occasions when High Court injunctions limiting protest soon followed after NGOs had joined in campaigns and performed various actions.

At this point, other national campaigners also suspicious of Rothery's and Daniels behaviour had researched them more, to find evidence of Rothery proclaiming to be one of the orgainsers of Occupy LSX protests on the mainstream media news outlet CNBC, some five years earlier. Watching it on YouTube, I knew that for someone claiming she was simply a concerned grandmother, a novice to campaigning before fracking, she was far too eloquent and professional in her approach and presentation. This went much deeper, than I had previously thought. The previous injunction on protest at PNR, obtained in October 2014, had expired in October 2016, so many of us wondered if RTP and Occupy coming up that weekend would result in another injunction. Of course, we were right, and always one step ahead, at this point.

We had witnessed Rothery's manipulative behaviour for six-weeks now and had concluded that if Rothery and her team were really interested in disrupting Cuadrilla, they could have occupied the site between October 2016 and February 2017, when there was no injunction in place (Cuadrilla started work the first week in January 2017) as she claimed she would in 2014. More importantly, why do this upcoming occupation now when activists were on top? Why not wait until later, when we were not? Was this planned occupation agreed with the police and Cuadrilla to obtain evidence for an injunction stopping further genuine protest on public land? Was Rothery gaslighting the social media world, claiming she was resisting Cuadrilla to hide the underlying issue of the inevitable injunction incoming? These were just some of the questions that many of us were asking at this time. We knew she was working with the police, but what we did not know, was who was paying her to do so: was it the Green Party, Greenpeace, NGOs, trade unions, private individuals, intelligence services or the fracking industry itself?

Sixteen

The First Cuadrilla
High Court Injunction

ON SATURDAY 25TH February, a group of about 150 people gathered at John Tootill's Maple Farm, some six hundred metres west of the drilling site on the same A583. Tootill's garden centre business was about fifty yards further down a lane at the back of where his roadside anti-fracking billboards were situated. The roadside area was generally unused, so he allowed activists to use it, for charging phones, water etc. During the gathering, people spoke to the crowd until Logic Al concluded by whipping up the group of people enough to encourage them to storm the field around the drilling site perimeter, ripping down heras fencing in front of gates leading up to drill site in the process. Had Rothery put him up to it? He was, after all, one of her team, and Daniels had attempted to recruit locals to help take the field a week or so earlier.

I stayed away knowing something was afoot, and watched events on a livestream from my home. Rothery looked delighted once Logic Al had given his speech; she didn't take part in the taking of the field, she simply watched the events unfold before walking off into the distance with a smile on her face. Dan Evans, the guy from Occupy who had twice backed out of previous actions in 2014, rattled the fencing and roused the crowd before the fencing broke. I observed in amazement as police helped people onto the field by supporting them over fences. Police don't usually help activists take an area for occupation; this was out-of-the-ordinary. The occupation lasted a short-time, whilst people danced about on the field, before realising the support promised by Rothery and Daniels had not materialised. People in attendance had been told RTP and Occupy would be joining them in the occupation. No one was arrested during this brief occupation, but the evidence was provided for at the very least a land injunction.

What was this action all about? Was it a chance for Cuadrilla or the police to gather intelligence of who was prepared to do Rothery's bidding? Or was it designed purely to create the evidence for a new injunction, with previous one, now ended? I could not work it out. Add to this the increased online attacks myself and many other activists were now receiving, and it felt to me we were in the middle of a psychological operation (Psyops) to slander many activists' good names and undo all the hard work we'd done fighting off the frackers the previous years.

Suddenly, one particular individual (a troll) called Florence Gate (social media name) appeared online, yet no activist I knew had ever met her. Unsurprisingly, we soon realised she was connected to one of Rothery's cohorts in Frack Free Lancashire, Nick Danby. Many of us were now denounced as anti-semitic, transphobic or misogynist in an attempt to discredit us further and turn other campaigners against us. So now, because I questioned Rothery's motives, I was a misogynist. I suspected those involved believed if they could get away slurs on Jeremy Corbyn, they could easily target lesser knowns. Supporting the struggles of the Palestinian people, does not make one anti-semitic. As for the transphobic labels, from a personal point of view, what other people describe themselves as is not my business, I was just concerned with stopping fracking. This made me concerned for the wider anti-fracking movement, because I could see their agenda. I just tackled them as I tackled the frackers, continuing to call them out and oppose their destructive ways. It was not easy though as Rothery had a large social media audience because of the £55,000 case only months earlier, affiliation to the Green Party, mainstream NGOs, and god only knows who else.

The online damage this troll Gate did to the reputations of many activists locally and nationally was so severe, she was undoubtedly a professional. I was campaigning online for many hours over those previous four years and I never witnessed anything that came close to this psychological warfare. Gate had only appeared online occasionally in the early months of the PNR campaign. Now, she cleverly created a 'secret' group on social media for 'admins and moderators' of local anti-fracking groups around the country, and set out to manipulate various admins on those groups. Soon, none of these 'admins' of local groups would be allowing campaign details and vital evidence of what was occurring at PNR on their pages, hypocritically claiming it was divisive. What we had now uncovered about Rothery and her cohorts in Lancashire meant that, for grassroots campaigning to survive, it needed containing in Lancashire and not spreading everywhere else. Of course, the operation we were now up against was increasing its resources by the day, so were fighting a losing battle.

Gate was not alone in her online operation. Logic and his girlfriend Sally Moss took over as administrators on several Facebook groups and if they couldn't control the narrative, they blocked local people out of their own campaign groups. Causing division and diverting energy away from stop fracking was the name of the game. To me, it was clear that the movement was awash with agents and actors stirring up trouble, damaging reputations and destroying the solidarity we had created over the years. It revealed a weakness in using social media for grassroots campaigning, if someone from outside the area could take over information sharing so easily and on a national scale. Still, it showed us what collectively we were now up against, spirit-destroying psychological abuse, as well as any drilling rig and fracking company. My personal Twitter account, the following week, was full of friend requests from intelligence services, mostly in the US. I suspected this was an attempt to generate fear in me, but I just blocked them straight away.

Challenging Cuadrilla's Protest Pen

One week after the short occupation of the field next to PNR drill site, Cuadrilla issued court papers to the PNR fracking site heras fencing, addressed to 'persons unknown' and the third defendant from the 2014 case - Rothery. However, what Rothery, Cuadrilla and the police were not to know is that a team of seven of us were to work on these court papers all weekend. One of our team was the most respected campaigner in Lancashire Bob Dennett, who had campaigned against fracking for years and had attended our meeting in Huddersfield years earlier. He and Ebony, who had both founded FFL, had now given up the reins after pressure from certain others.

The rest of us taking on the court case challenge were a small group of educated people who could understand the legal papers, had sound knowledge of protesting on the front lines, and were able to prepare a defence to the deceit, in a very short time. I expected many in the community thought FFL would stand up given that they were getting thousands of pounds from locals to support the resistance, with some high-up connections in various professions. Would FFL build a challenge? Would the climate NGOs make an appearance and challenge?

What we uncovered that weekend was a real turning point in our awareness of what we were up against. In the court papers for this new injunction application for Cuadrilla was a new requirement that protestors be put in a pen, just like sheep are put in. We couldn't believe it. If granted, it would set the precedent through civil law for the industry and all councils to box everyone into one area to protest on private land, or face arrest. The pen itself was to be twenty-five by twenty-five metres, behind a hedge on a field one hundred metres from the fracking site. The police and Cuadrilla were trying to get people to wave their banners from this area only.

Our team worked hard on a skeleton argument, and Ian Crane was to be our representative in the court. We had no intention of challenging the injunction's trespassing part; we reluctantly agreed it would continue after its previous successful two years. Instead, our central argument would focus on resisting the pen because we knew the lasting implications of that for rights to protest on public land everywhere, not just here.

The morning of the hearing, we arrived at the Civil Court in Manchester early to put the final preparations of our skeleton paperwork and forty pages of supporting submissions together. Plus, we wanted to avoid the crowd of nanas, climate change campaigners and the usual media circus that appeared when anything involved Rothery - as in her 2014 and 2016 court appearances.

After completing our final assignments, I went outside with Wayne Paolucci and Dennett for a cigarette; the other four, Ian Crane, Ben Dean, Sharon Whale and John Ozric, stayed in the ground floor café. As we departed the building, we were expecting a sea of campaigners in the yellow and black anti-fracking colours, and other banner-waving climate NGOs. Instead, the only person outside was a local independent photographer called Dave Ellison, whom we had met many times in the previous years at campaign gatherings and camps. He was as surprised as us that no one was there.

The next minute, a car pulls up out of nowhere, and Rothery gets out of the back, alone. *Where is her entourage?* I thought. *Not even one other nana? Wait till she sees us...*

We saw the shock in the photographer's face when she marched up to him and, just ten-metres from where we were standing, said, "What the fuck are they doing here?"

Of course, the photographer had no idea; we had long been following an array of issues within the hierarchical Lancashire campaign and were there to try our best to railroad their strategic plans. Although a lot of our time was regrettably taken up deflecting trolls online and trying to maintain our psychological well-being in the face of all the gaslighting and manipulation, we were still able to focus on such an important issue as this. Rothery's arrogance revealed that she thought our team of experienced social and environmental justice campaigners were total idiots. It would be her downfall.

After Rothery entered the building, we did the same, to join the others before heading to the courtroom. She looked even more surprised to see the other four, as well. The expletives continued when our team gave our defence papers to the court usher.

"What the fuck are they doing here?' she said in the general direction of the court usher, before swearing some more. We clearly had her rattled, so she phoned a Mackenzie friend who none of us knew.

The case began with Ian Crane applying to the Judge to join the proceedings on all our behalf. He was not named on the documents but could become a party to the proceedings as a 'person unknown', just as Rothery had in 2014. Ian gave Cuadrilla's lawyer, Rothery and Judge Raynor QC the skeleton argument we had prepared. We didn't expect Cuadrilla's lawyer to allow this; after all, their lawyer probably assumed this event would be a mere formality given that he hadn't even brought a team with him. This absence was in stark contrast to the 2014 injunction case when there were three or four rows of their backroom team. Did Cuadrilla know Rothery was not going to be legally represented in advance?

Apart from Ben, who was Ian's Mackenzie friend, so stayed next to him, we spread out all over the court. Thankfully, the Judge gave Ian ten minutes to explain our position, but he wanted Ian to contest everything (the pen and trespass), so Ian stepped out. We had all agreed that the trespass injunction was inevitable and our only concern was the pen. The risk of heavy court costs was a risk not worth taking under these circumstances.

The Judge then asked asked Rothery if she wanted to contest everything given that she was the named defendant. There was a long silence before Crane leaned back in his chair to look at Rothery, nod and mouth, 'Yes, yes, you do want to contest everything, surely?' Bob Dennett, sitting behind Rothery, was also saying the same. I was just astounded that she wasn't quick to contest. If she said no, we'd have witnessed her stitching us all up. So she eventually said yes.

The Judge proceeded, and Rothery began her usual gambit about being a grandmother, explaining why it was wrong to give the injunction. But she had very little to say about the pen. The Judge was not interested in this grandmother's gaslighting and swiftly moved her on. Furiously flustered, Rothery banged on the desk with her rolled up court papers, and claimed she was in Scandinavia so had not had time to read the papers until she had returned.

The Judge then offered her an adjournment to seek legal advice, which she refused. Was her objective to have protests controlled at Little Plumpton immediately? Any legal professional would have made a strong case to oppose the pen. We had, and it was not any of our professions, so why didn't she accept the offer? Over the hearing's lunchtime break, Judge Raynor QC possibly read our skeleton arguments, highlighting the difference between the previous 2014 injunction and this new one (the pen) and how crowding people into a pen was dangerous. Thankfully, when he made his decision that afternoon, Judge Raynor refused the protest pen.

Rothery was livid and banged her hand on the bench, her face turning a shade of purple. I knew then that she was there to give Cuadrilla and the police what they wanted. It made sense of her lack of entourage, and we found out later she had insisted she attend alone. This way there would be no witnesses or opposition in the courtroom, as she was not expecting us. Someone (persons unknown) could have stood up in court and opposed the proposals once they had heard about the pen, just as she had raised her arm in 2014. So her going in alone limited this chance.

Locals later told us that Rothery had been trying to convince them a pen would be a great place to protest from. Telling folk they could decorate the pen and have cake and tea safely there. If locals wanted to go in the pen, I was not against it, but I had no intention of being penned in for my protest. The idea was an afront to my civil liberties and everyone else's, not just anti-fracking campaigners. Why was she pushing for a pen before the court papers were even released though?

Cuadrilla had not even turned up with solicitors on their benches, they'd seen it as a formality on all counts. And Rothery's lackadaisical attitude to this hearing belied her motives to control our protest. I suspected she simply went there that day to have her name removed from injunction, whilst Cuadrilla and the police got their pen. We knew anything was possible now and had a feeling there might be further strategic plans ahead in the denial of rights to protest, after their collective failure here. In fact, what we had just witnessed, was only the beginning of an orchestrated attack on our human rights to protest.

Back at the Cuadrilla drilling site gates, any local community member who tried to voice concerns to Rothery or her sister Daniels about their motives now faced a targeted gaslighting and intimidation program, in an attempt to force them away. God only knows what she was telling locals off-screen because it materialised that she and her team could divide families so much, they would not speak until after Cuadrilla's operation ended. This first-class psychological abuse was a familiar theme at PNR, but the wider community were none the wiser, with no idea it was Rothery and Daniels who led the way. It didn't help that the local and national media, especially the Blackpool Gazette and the Guardian, gave her the dominant voice, but they had seen to that by recruiting Stephenson as FFL media spokesperson.

I stayed at the camp of New Hope for about a week, but did not feel welcome around these people, especially McCann and a new member called Jag Wag. The energies they were giving off together was one of dark pasts that was still present. McCann had been at Barton Moss and Upton, but I had become wary of him ever since he had caused considerable unrest between the camp and that community. But here he was again, doing the same thing, stirring up trouble. I was not fearful of these people many of us soon after called actorvists, because I knew in the grand scheme of things, they were only low-level police or industry fodder. On a scale of one to ten, these people were no higher than about two, even if they thought they were an eleven. On the same scale, I'd say Rothery and Daniels were about eight, because in no way could they be achieving this type of operation without direct contact with the authorities. It was almost as if these people were untouchable, and these actorvists would often say just that.

Not wanting to be around these new camp members any longer, I left quickly, not even packing up my tent, which I had paid two-hundred-pounds for the previous summer. For me, the further away from this place the better, for my spiritual, emotional and psychological well-being. Thankfully, I was still attending my Gamblers Anonymous meetings, so I was able to stay mentally strong and resilient despite all the negativity being flung at me from all angles, but it was a tough time emotionally.

Happily back home, I monitored tactics from livestreams on social media but kept in daily contact with local community members. Soon after, McCann and Yellowbelly headed up New Hope and joined forces with Rothery, convening 'consensus meetings' that were anything but that. One example was when they held a meeting on local anti-fracking farmer John Tootill's nearby land at Maple Farm about who they wanted to bar from the 'community hub' situated there and funded by those who wanted to stop fracking.

Sue Marshall, who was at the meeting said, "Tootill didn't want Geza or me to be barred, and said so." But his land or not, it didn't hold any sway once Yellowbelly started hand-waving and gesticulating support as the list of the soon to be barred activists was being read out. For Marshall, "the hand-waving was stomach-churning to watch." I knew all about consensus meetings and how they operated, from an Occupy event in Parliament Square that I attended in October 2014, before I started becoming suspicious of their motives. Stooges amongst the people gathered react enthusiastically to suggestions being made, and by strategically placing themselves in the audience they sway the consensus of opinion and gave the illusion of democaracy in action.

Marshall explained further that, "other hand-wavers indicated their support too, whilst Daniels and Rothery feigned looks of surprise as they looked around the room supposedly assessing the 'democratic' decision to bar all those that they had, in fact, decided they wanted barring the day before the meeting was held."

This happened over and over again to anyone expressing concern or dissent against any of Rothery's or her cohorts' decisions to control and prohibit protest, which led to many genuinely concerned local people becoming slandered and excommunicated. Being seen to like a Facebook post of someone after they had been barred or excommunicated could result in you being excluded and blocked from groups and information across the country. The control was so pernicious and got so bad that even the locals who built and set up the first gate camp at PNR were excluded from participating, denied any information and barred from sitting in the shelter that they had built.

Many locals now stopped communicating with Rothery and the rest of the FFL hierarchy because they also knew something bigger was taking place. It was always the local campaigners who would have cameras rammed in their faces by the likes of McCann and John O'Connor while they were outside the site protesting. The police would then threaten the local with arrest or tell them to move away. It was so blatant and McCann and O'Connor became known as 'Tina's bitches' by locals. The police tried to look independent but there were key people there who they simply left alone; so it was obvious who and what they were protecting. The police operation appeared to be to eradicate all grassroots resistance to Cuadrilla at Little Plumpton, unless it was agreed protest with Rothery and Daniels.

I knew all about informants and how they operated, from being raised in a built-up area where it was not uncommon to hear people being called a *grass* if they gave information to the police. The difference here was that these people were acting blatantly in public, surprising locals how they were able to get away with their actions, incuding physically attacking people and breaking community members' phones. If these people were the general public, they would have been arrested for assault, breach of the peace, intimidation and harassment. But the police would never arrest any 'actorvists', they would simply tell them to move on or even arrest the locals being harassed by them, instead.

One thing that was obvious from my livestream observations: you could see the shift changes in actorvists taking place every four to six weeks. One group would leave the area, and a similar number would appear. Kieran Dunne, Yellowbelly and McCann, were the obvious three, time and time again. Locals would post on social media with delight when these actorvists publicly announced they were leaving PNR, to be later disappointed when others would return. These people were from all over the country, yet the authorities did not treat them as national activists. New Hope was renamed No Hope by the locals who were genuinely only interested in stopping the fracking site and the number of ex-convicts/criminals on the camp who were in Rothery's entourage was noted.

I also watched a weekly, successful, grassroots-organised protest day organised by a fabulous northern campaigner Victoria Aeyn get hijacked by Rothery and her crew. Swap Work for Work Wednesdays involved local people swapping work for the day, to protest instead (called work for work because of the amount of times people would be shouted at to 'get a job'). This masterful event was seeing PNR swarming with local people, effectively resisting the industry. But then, some weeks later, Rothery destroyed these days by starting the Women in White protests on the same day, where women only would gather at the gates wearing white, a colour of peace they said, but also of course, the colour of surrender. These weekly protests divided the locals because one was seen as lawful (managed) by authorities (Women in White) and the other (Swap Work) unlawful (unmanaged). This appeared to be a clear 'divide and conquer' technique designed by specialists and implemented again by Rothery and Daniels.

I doubted they could plan so many strategic operations on their own. How many people were working with them, or directing them from the authorities? At this point, we had no idea. All I knew was that I would never go back to PNR because it was far too damaging and I could be far more effective watching it all unfold, whilst moving forward with other campaigns. After all, the world never ended at PNR and there was still more work to be done elsewhere.

Seventeen

Taking the Protest to the Fracking Supply Chain

DURING THE MONTHS that followed in 2017, I followed my conscience once more. When you're protesting on the front line at drilling sites, you start to see where all the haulage companies involved are based and where all the site equipment comes from. One such company was the Marriott Drilling Group, based in Clay Cross, Chesterfield, North East Derbyshire. This onshore deep drilling company had leased their rig to Dart Energy back in 2014 to drill exploratory coal bed methane boreholes at Farndon and Daneshill.

Despite Marriott denying it, we knew that some of Cuadrilla's equipment was stored there, from their earlier wells drilled and fracked at other sites in Lancashire in 2011. But we were unsure whether the Cuadrilla rig at Marriott was the one Cuadrilla would be using at PNR. We were taking no chances and believed its movement needed monitoring. Then we could alert trusted Lancashire campaigners if any equipment left there heading for Little Plumpton.

In a livestream at PNR in the previous days, we (myself and Sharon) had seen equipment going into the site, that looked like it must be coming from the Marriott Drilling Company. So, the two of us and Ben, decided to take a trip over there and check it out for ourselves. Of course, the FFL hierarchy had told the community they had it all under control, but that never satisfied us. Every piece of equipment that went in Cuadrilla's drill site was a step closer to fracking, and they certainly could not be trusted to disrupt it, as the previous weeks had shown.

The Marriott headquarters is on a small industrial estate, with a railway line to the rear and a ditch with a running stream next to the fence. As soon as we drove towards the depot, we saw two drilling rigs standing high above the estate at the front, one being Cuadrilla's, which had already operated elsewhere in Lancashire. We decided to take a walk around the site perimeter and see what was happening inside.

It looked as if equipment that was to be heading to Lancashire was in the process of being loaded on the back of a lorry from a company we had seen at Barton Moss and PNR previously. Coincidentally, that company was called Boyd Haulage, based in Buxton. I remembered this company for obvious reasons and the fact that the driver drove into campaigners at Barton Moss.

We were soon confronted by a local business owner and his family, who stormed out of their premises to the rear of Marriott, and faced me in an intimidating manner. I held firm, undeterred, with a camera in my hand, and then two Police Community Support Officers (PCSOs) arrived. We were not breaking any laws, so the PCSOs left shortly after. We then walked around the premises to wait for the lorry to come out, because we had already decided to exercise our right to protest. I would slow-walk the vehicle to the top of the estate on my own, as Ben was driving and Sharon was filming,

After a short confrontation with another business owner next door and the Managing Director of Marriott, who went by the name of Jonathon Hobday (Jonti), my right to protest was not denied. By now, real coppers had turned up, so they took control and facilitated it all in a peaceful manner, which took about twenty minutes in total. Of course, the driver and Jonti both refuted the lorry's destination, but we were reasonably sure where it was going. We let some trusted local campaigners know that it was heading their way, and sure enough about three hours later, it turned up at PNR. Just as the lorry was about to enter the site, a campaigner John Knox (Knoxy), jumped on top for a lorry surf, like I had witnessed at Barton Moss years earlier, successfully holding it up even longer. Sue, John's mother, another scouser, was a regular at anti-fracking camps and had been for many years.

Realising we were onto something at Marriott's, campaigners set up a protection camp that night, some fifty-metres from their front entrance. It was on land owned by the Worcester Bosch group, who had witnessed our protest earlier that day. The Bosch Group is a very environmentally conscious business with ninety five percent of profits going to charities. So a couple of campaigners arranged a meeting with the boss to explain what we were doing. Sitting in their plush leather chairs in their meeting room drinking coffee, he heard us out and allowed us to stay, as long as we were respectful.

Once we were there and broadcasting our slow-walk protests, the local community started to join us, peacefully protesting in the same way. Florence Gate had appeared not to have infiltrated this group, no doubt because these campaigners, knew all too well of what can happen during a campaign, with raw memories of times during the miners' strikes in those parts. Some of the most determined and committed activists I've met (too many to mention) resided in this part of the country and would be regular welcome visitors. We felt that sense of unity amongst activists again, able to protest freely while still disrupting Cuadrilla's operations and not be targeted by Lancashire Police.

The Marriott protest was also a step forward for the anti-fracking campaign in Derbyshire because their area was under threat from the country's biggest shale licence holder INEOS, an international petrochemicals company with a widely-reported terrible track record on environmental pollution, detailed in research by Food and Water Watch Europe. INEOS, owned by the UK's then richest man Jim Ratcliffe, had acquired over one million acres of land through Petroleum Exploration Development Licence's (PEDLs) to explore shale gas prospects throughout Northern England, including sites at Marsh Lane in Derbyshire and Woodsetts and Harthill in South Yorkshire. They also have a share in some of the IGas sites in the East Midlands. They were keen on fracking to obtain the by-products of shale gas for their plastic-producing plants – a realisation that turned the mainstream media and government narrative of shale gas being for homes on its head. All while the government was declaring a war on plastics!

The initial weeks of the protest involved slow-walking a large convoy of seismic survey pick-up trucks from the gates of Marriott Drilling to the top road, some fifty metres away. These seismic survey operations link to fracking and other industries by mapping the geology underground in 3D, so warranted slowing down. We were always courteous to the other industrial site businesses and ensured we still left one side of the road clear for them. The police could have just sent a couple of police officers to facilitate the protest, as they had with my one-person demonstration earlier, but often there were slightly more coppers than protestors. Mind you, apart from one incident when a woman was shoved to the ground, widely reported in mainstream news, I found Derbyshire Constabulary by far the least aggressive force I'd dealt with.

However, one Saturday morning, I was slow-walking a large trailer with some equipment on, when about ten coppers turned up. I was then pushed and shoved by two of them before they arrested me out of the blue for Section Five of the Public Order Act. The charge against me was later dropped, sometime between arrest and first court appearance, although I was uninformed. But it didn't stop me continuing to protest there along with many others.

Eighteen

Rolling Resistance -
Stopping Fracking or Stopping Protest?

THROUGHOUT JULY 2017, RTP's Rolling Resistance came to Lancashire and Derbyshire with a month of various direct actions 'apparently' designed to cause as much disruption to the fracking industry as possible. This month became hugely significant in the UK's fight against fracking, for many reasons. It began with the official unveiling of the Maple Farm Community Hub, an information point for finding out about fracking. Frank Roberts a veteran of Barton Moss had camped there during the early months, to stay away from of the alcohol side of things on the larger New Hope camp. However, Frank was targeted because of his livestreaming and Logic was heard feeding information to the police about him. Knowing he was being set up, he left and was a great loss to those locals who really valued him. This included his efforts to motivate those on camp to actually get out of bed in the morning and up to the site to protest. Now it had been taken over by Rothery and FFL, and national and local activists were calling it Lancashire Constabulary Fracking HQ.

The Rolling Resistance month included lock-ons, die-ins, a bike ride from Manchester to Blackpool, and various other events to highlight what was happening at PNR and to supposedly stop the drill from being delivered any time soon. One of the first direct actions in front of the gates of the Cuadrilla drilling site that month was a thirteen-person lock-on involving three councillors Julie Brickles on Cuadrillas Community Liaison Group (CLG), Miranda Cox (CLG), Gina Dowding (was Green MEP), and joined by the retired civil servant of FFL, Nick Danby. They set up at three o' clock in the morning and after a long day of lying on the concrete and being cut out by the specialist police team, they were all arrested and charged with obstructing a public highway and offences under Section 241 of the Trades Union and Labour Relations Consolidation Act.

Later that same afternoon, after the arrests of the councillors, some of the actorvists revealed their position to the local community in broad daylight. Campaigners had built two towers on either side of the site's gates to monitor Cuadrilla from a higher point. Local campaigners had possession of each structure until the actorvists Lee Walsh and Fargo McCann somehow deceived those occupying that they would take over. Both then left the towers, before McCann nodded to police that they were empty. Hood up to cover his face, he then tried to slide away, but was caught on film. The police then gained control, much to the annoyance of a local activist Bibbs, who had seen the manoeuvre and tried to regain it. Police then held him and another campaigner back, before he was then violently arrested by police. Within fifteen minutes of this happening, a local demolition firm with a JCB was on the scene. It was clear they were all working together because the JCB was waiting around the corner for the all-clear. The trailer it was carried on passed the site empty just minutes earlier. At this point, locals already had suspicions about McCann being an informant, as they had witnessed him going on early morning expeditions to Penny Farm, the farm opposite Maple Farm, where the police would have a base for their operations.

At court, later in the year, the councillors were all found guilty of obstructing the highway and not guilty of the Trade Union Act, receiving a twelve-month conditional discharge and ordered to pay costs and surcharges amounting to £270. This verdict was strange, considering the two councillors were part of Cuadrilla's Community Liaison Group. This outcome was even more odd because a group of ten Greenpeace activists who had undertaken a similar group lock-on with giant yellow boxes, two months earlier, were all acquitted when their case got to court. The Greenpeace direct action was almost identical to that of the councillors.

At the trial in November 2017, it was District Judge Brailsford who found the Greenpeace activists not guilty. However, earlier in the year, he had also found myself and three other campaigners guilty of the same charge as the councillors and Greenpeace, doing the exact same thing, sitting calmly and peacefully locked on to each other in front of the PNR gates. What was the difference? With the Greenpeace defendants, Brailsford decided that they held 'genuine beliefs' and were entitled to express those beliefs. Furthermore, they apparently had a 'lawful excuse' for their protest. Didn't others doing similar actions have the same lawful excuse? Or are only NGO activists entitled to hold 'genuine beliefs' and express those beliefs without a criminal charge?

A week after that thirteen-person lock-on involving councillors, three-generations of a family took direct action. With a lot of police already at the gates, a vehicle drove up and six activists got out these huge green boxes, similar to those of Greenpeace two months earlier, right under the noses of the coppers, and locked on through them. Meanwhile, Cuadrilla security and Rothery's team of actorvists were throwing each other about to cause chaos and confusion while the campaigners sat down, all livestreamed to the world. As I watched from home, I could not work out how, with multiple police forces and security there, they managed to drive big green blocks on a vehicle to the site unnoticed in broad daylight. It looked like it had been allowed to happen as planned. After another day of effectively blocking the site, the protestors were arrested and charged as usual with obstructing a public highway, and then also found guilty at trial in January 2018.

The following morning, at the gates of the Marriott Drilling depot, RTP activists staged a tri-pod blockade, holding up traffic going in and out of Marriott's for the day. With our slow-walking, we'd always been careful to leave one lane for other businesses to come and go, but this precarious direct action enabled police to close the whole road on safety grounds, because the little room left for passing lorries was dangerous. I couldn't help but see a pattern emerging of this particular NGO's actions being the catalyst for injunctions restricting the right to protest and the denial of grassroots resistance, thereby disenfranchising people who felt compelled to protest beyond the normal one day or week of action.

From what I had experienced I could see that people needed to feel as if they affect the issue they are campaigning against; otherwise, what is the point in demonstrating? Once local democracy has failed, being able to use your body to disrupt is the only option you have left. This is very empowering, otherwise we can simply sign a petition or wave a banner and achieve the same outcome, nothing. Some may think the democratic representative system is the best option for change, but the tiny percentage of petition success or politicians acting according to what their constituents want, paints a different picture. And when the national government overrules local democracy, the only solution is to get in the way of that decision and make your views known through consistent, long-term protest.

Over a week later, I was arrested for a second time at Marriott – my eighth arrest with only two convictions, so far - again while a group of us were slow-walking a vehicle in to the site. Many other campaigners were also arrested, so we suspected this was an attempt to clear the camp. We were all bundled into vans and cars and taken to Chesterfield Police Station. I was in custody for around twenty-hours, which is by far the longest of any arrests. I was not happy at all about my arrest and felt the coppers were stitching me up, to bail me away as the other forces had. I spent the time in the cell reading and exercising to pass the hours. My time in custody was not going to deter me in the future though, it just made me more determined. As a condition of our release, we were all bailed away from North East Derbyshire until we had our bail conditions removed weeks later.

Back at PNR, directly outside Maple Farm, at about eight o' clock in the morning on the twenty-fifth of July, the first of what would be several lorry surfers connected to RTP, Richard Roberts, climbed a lorry heading for the drill site. Almost simultaneously, a second campaigner Rich Loizou scaled a lorry, and a third person joined them mid-aftertoon. The three became four when another campaigner Julian Brock, not affiliated with RTP, or any other group, joined them in the early hours of the twenty-sixth of July. Loizou ended his protest first, some forty five hours later, Blevins seventy-three hours from the beginning and Roberts, eighty-four hours after he started the action. The final person was Brock, ninety-nine hours after the action had begun, with him lasting seventy-six hours. All four were charged with what was a 'new protest charge of public nuisance'. This new protest charge was bad news for further protests of a similar nature because in other previous case precedents it carried a custodial sentence.

Despite all this action just down the road from the gates of the Cuadrilla shale gas exploration site, on the morning of the twenty-seventh of July, I woke to the news that the rig to drill the first two horizontal wells in UK shale rock had arrived. According to Lancashire Constabulary's record of the fracking industry's private security operation, they had facilitated delivery of the drilling rig at Cuadrilla's site at four o'clock in the morning, very much outside the hours of working as specified by their planning permission. Lancashire County Council said they investigated the breach, and would put in measures to prevent a recurrence. What a pointless response: the rig was in.

Many locals who had been resisting Cuadrilla believed the lorry surfing stunt was the perfect distraction. There was no resistance to the rig's entrance because everyone had been at Maple Farm with their attention turned to the lorry surfers, while the FFL hierarchy had gone home for the night. We'll never know whether if there had been no lorry surfing there might have been a presence at the gates. So much for a rolling resistance from Rothery and RTP again though.

However, what occurred on the final day of the rolling resistance month would shock me and many other campaigners in Northern England even more. At a secret hearing at the High Court in London on the thirty-first of July, INEOS was granted a wide-ranging injunction seriously limiting people's right to protest against their activities and those of companies linked to them. These proceedings took place without anyone knowing, with vast amounts of evidence provided to show an 'real and imminent threat' to INEOS's business.

No one knew their lawyers at Field Fishers had been collating over thirty lever-arch files, and six-hours of video footage, of historical evidence of camps occupying land and, of course, the last few months of demonstrations ramping up with the Rolling Resistance. Basically, this was an attempt to criminalise protest, before protest has even taken place against INEOS. With so much damning evidence of disruption on public land, Justice Morgan presiding over the case, couldn't fail to be overwhelmed by all the evidence presented showing a 'real and imminent threat' even if he only had a few hours to make his decision.

When we heard the news of this injunction, the first of its kind, Ian Crane, Helen Chuntso, Benjamin Dean, Sharon Whale and I looked at its detail and were shocked by how wide-ranging it was. It was by far the most draconian attack on protests rights seen in modern times. We knew at once we must challenge it, at a High Court hearing set for the twelth of September. Not only was this a protest-stifling UK issue, but it was also a game-changing global matter. And we would do our utmost to stop it.

Once my bail conditions were yet again removed, I returned back to camp at Marriott. The police operation was now a zero-tolerance approach at the site, stopping slow-walks and only allowing protestors to stand outside the gates and wave a banner for twenty minutes, whilst vehicles sat waiting to exit the depot. Workers would just eat their lunch and have a drink, waiting for the clock to tick down: it was useless. One could not help feel that the closing of the road weeks earlier had led to the change in police tactics. *Thanks, RTP*, I thought. *We were doing alright here without your 'help'.*

Nineteen

Building a Case to Challenge the INEOS Injunction

THE GRASSROOTS PROTEST movement was at a critical juncture. If nobody was to challenge this draconian INEOS injunction, then slow walking, even on a public pavement outside a protest site, would mean certain arrest for breaching the terms. Protestors could face contempt of court charges making us liable for up to six months imprisonment and / or a fine of up to £5000. It couldn't be allowed to happen, but would we even get legal representation to fight it?

It appeared there was no one else stepping up to contest it, in particular the NGOs. It seemed the INGO-led climate change movement were happy to wave banners and sign petitions but were not interested in defending people's rights to protest, in person, to protect the environment. A strange reality considering how much they were saying we were in a 'climate emergency' and, therefore, oil and gas drilling needed to be stopped.

All I could see was the end to everybody's right to lawful protest. I suspected the case law would also be used to build corporations' defense against protests in other countries, maybe not right away but over time, especially as most businesses are cross-boundary under globalisation. In this way, no national government would have to rewrite legislation and be seen as authoritarian. Any government, particularly the British, that like to be seen as democratic and promoting human rights, could continue to appear reasonable, without the majority of the population knowing, while civil court injunctions such as this stopped any real democracy taking place. Authoritarianism through the back door, if you like.

So, Ian Crane, Helen Chuntso and I started discussing our options and began to organise a challenge. I had known Helen since Barton Moss when supporting us as part of Frack Free Greater Manchester, she would often come to camp with her young children. Helen lived in Greater Manchester, but was from Liverpool originally, so we both had that scouse spirit running through our veins and a sense of solidarity. While I was at the Barton Moss camp, I went with her and Rachel Thompson to an open day with the law firm Leigh Day in London, to find out more about public and environmental law and how they could be of help if needed. Sometimes you have no idea why the universe is sending you somewhere, but now forty months later I realised why, as we were still in touch and able to use that legal firm's assistance.

Three of us were willing to challenge this injunction as a group, but the law firm decided there could only be one of us. Helen had a family so wasn't one of the three. Myself, Ian and a local in Kirby Misperton, put our names forward. Ian was seen as a journalist and the gentlemen from Kirby Misperton had little experience of the previous years of the anti-fracking movement, so the legal team asked if would I take it on.

As an experienced campaigner both on the front lines and in researching, I knew I would be able to pull together the evidence needed to support a challenge, so accepted the proposal. Nevertheless, it was hard to believe that less than four years earlier, I had been close to death, and now, here I was challenging the richest man in Britain (at the time) on behalf of all grassroots campaigners. I had no assets, but what I did have was guts and an in-depth knowledge of the anti-fracking protests, which would be vital to the legal team building our case in a short amount of time.

For the next ten days, I worked alongside the Leigh Day solicitors and barristers Heather Williams QC, a leading human rights lawyer, and Blinne Ní Ghrálaigh, also a human rights expert on protest and international law. I spent many hours working long into the night, compiling answers to multiple questions from my legal team about anti-fracking protests and the movement's history. I didn't go into any suspicions about NGO infiltration and manipulation, this wasn't the time. But any questions about grassroots anti-fracking activism I could answer factually and in detail. I had lived and breathed the campaign for nearly four years, in between study, which, in perfect synchronicity, I had just finished two weeks earlier, freeing me up to work on this huge challenge.

A real boost for me came when Jennifer Robinson, solicitor to Julian Assange, also joined the legal team, making me fully realise how serious our case was. I had known about the extradition of Julian Assange case for many years, and now his solicitor was helping defend our rights to protest. Jennifer told me she had read about our case and was immediately shocked, so she contacted Heather and asked how she could help. How could all leading human rights professionals see the importance of challenging, whilst NGOs stayed silent?

Our argument at the forthcoming hearing centred around the terms of the interim injunction breaching Articles 10 and 11 of the European Convention on Human Rights, which guarantee the right to freedom of expression and freedom of association. By putting myself forward as the named defendant in those proceedings, I wanted to ensure that we as local people, citizens and campaigners still had the right to hold peaceful protests against the fracking industry and those involved in it, plus any other issue that needed protesting against in the future. The injuction was dangerous because any business or authority could obtain one on the basis of future events.

The silence from just about every social and environmental justice NGO, from Greenpeace to Liberty, was deafening. Initially, I found this hard to understand. Some of these organisations were forever asking for money to protect human rights across the world, but now they were ignoring precisely that here in the UK. It seemed like a deliberate attempt to distance themselves from grassroots movements. Either they were fine with our rights to protests being removed, or the state had warned them off; after all, the recent decade had shown the third sector of NGOs, charities and other non-profit groups is a revolving door to government, through consensus and cooperation. Is this why these NGOs such as Greenpeace are free to take direct action, with no fear of conviction in the UK? Maybe they knew that this injunction was not aimed at them, but only at grassroots movements trying to make a difference in their local areas. Furthermore, no grassroots action means more public funding for them.

With only two weeks to prepare the case, we remained quiet about my legal challenge and stayed focused. At the same time, Rothery and her crew were telling people to ignore the injunction and not share any information about it. We could not overlook this dangerous assault on a critically diminishing democratic system. Anyone with an ounce of knowledge knew what would happen if we ignored it; it would be rubber-stamped forever and a day.

About a week in, Joe Corre, who had funded a lot of Rothery's campaigning, announced his challenge to the injunction through the mainstream media. I was surprised because he had little experience of the protests on the ground and he also funded Rothery. I knew Corre and his mother had attended the Occupy LSX protests, back in 2011, and they were both vocal climate change campaigners, but I had seen neither staying on camps or resisting the industry physically, other than for publicity. Yet here was Corre stepping in to fight the injunction – but only on a few points and making the clear distinction between allowing what he saw as lawful protest, such as managed protest, waving banners and signing petitions, and the rest deemed unlawful. As it was, this injunction wouldn't affect what they did; they could continue to use their wealth for supporting specific groups and for climate change awareness-raising regardless.

I questioned whether he stepped in to boost his ego, or that he hoped to get in first before anyone else challenged the injunction – as barely anyone knew I was taking it on - and he could steer it the way the controlled opposition wanted it, leading the way to limiting protest. Climate change campaigner Lorraine Inglis was building his case behind the scenes, evident from Freedom of Information requests at the time. Inglis is the climate change campaigner in the south, who is also spokesperson for the Weald Action Group and Frack Off London, which centralises the campaign narrative in southern England. Whatever Corre's reasons for joining, the fact he was also called Joe only raised the profile of the case, with 'Two Joes take on INEOS injunction' easy headlines in any media.

Unsurprisingly, when I announced my legal challenge in the days leading up to the court date, the FFL hierarchy instead of offering any support, started a smear campaign against me saying I was only doing it because of my ego. Who in their right mind would go through all this, two intense weeks of research and pressure, on behalf of all grassroots campaigners, just to boost their ego? I was exhausted and this was offensive. I just hoped their nonsense wouldn't have a negative effect on my national crowdfunding campaign for legal expenses.

I need not have worried. People worldwide were well aware of the dangers of this injunction against civil liberties and supported it wholeheartedly, donating over £17000 within two weeks of it becoming active. The first donation to the legal fund came from Victoria, who had organised the swap work day, again always on the side of humanity. I was blown away by the genuinely remarkable, collective response by everyday people, showing the faith people still had in me, despite the smear campaign. I had no financial help from any NGOs, political parties or wealthy private backers, it was all from regular people, like me, who could see the importance of what I was doing and wanted to help.

§

Tuesday the twelfth of September loomed and I was not especially hopeful of success at the High Court, as we were in a banker's court (civil division). This meant they were there to protect monetary interests. No surprise there. I knew I had the best human rights lawyers in the country, but corporations ruled in these types of courts. This was going to be tough: I was nervous but hopeful.

I met with Ian Crane outside and we had a short interview before we entered the building. As I was not representing the climate change NGO-led movement, there was no crowd outside just a couple of journalists, including Rob Evans of the Guardian and author of *Undercover*, mentioned earlier. Kevin Blowe of NETPOL and Nina Tailor of Gathering Place films were also outside but they were only concerned with speaking with Corre. Lack of communication with Tailor was unsurprising because she worked closely with Rothery and RTP, amongst others, and was filming at the Nana/RTP camp in 2014 and outside Preston County Hall in 2015 during Lancashire decision. Once inside, I had a brief discussion with the legal team on how the day would be approached, before entering the courtroom.

At this hearing, as expected, INEOS had sought a ruling making the injunction permanent, when no protesting had even taken place at their sites in Woodsetts, Harthill or Marsh Lane. The villages of Woodsetts and Harthill, only found out about the injunction when notices were installed around a field in their villages. However, Mr Justice Morgan, who had previously granted INEOS the injunction, decided to extend it for two months, with minor modifications, until a three-day hearing in November, which would then decide whether to impose it on a long-term basis or not. Corre was happy with the outcome, but I was disappointed. I knew further hard work, stress and court appearances would be necessary and spurred myself onwards.

Twenty

Team Effort to Kick the Frackers out of North Yorkshire

NEVER SHY OF a challenge and wanting to continue studying, I now embarked on an MSc in Public Health (Addictions) at the LJMU Public Health Institute in Liverpool, in September 2017. I could have continued postgraduate education with the Open University but I wanted to push myself further by attending university itself. Obviously, this was not the ideal time to start because of my involvement with the INEOS case, but I had already enrolled and set out my plans before they were awarded the injunction in July. Anyway, my personal life had to continue, so I decided to stick with it.

As it was, the legal team had advised me to take a less active role on the front line. I didn't need to go getting arrested right in the middle of this. But I hadn't anticipated how long the legal challenge would take, and felt gutted not to be able to get stuck into more protests, especially as things were hotting up at Third Energy's site at Kirby Misperton, North Yorkshire.

Police had now begun giving 'commanding orders' to campaigners to limit their protest in opposing Third Energy's plan to undertake the first high volume fracking in the UK since 2011. Work was set to start on the thirteenth of September, and already police were trying to normalise 'managed protest'. Anti-fracking campaigners denied any discussions about protest rules nor agreed to them. Similarly, those working in the background on the campaign, including councillors, denied these discussions. That's not to say climate change actors/agents were not in negotiations behind the community's back, because it was obvious by now that's how they operated.

In late 2016, before Cuadrillas' operations began at Little Plumpton, Richardson, Danby and Roberts from FFL visited Ian Crane, while he was staying long-term at the Kirby Misperton camp. They gave him a donation before trying to persuade him to negotiate with the police. Why would other campaigners do this? Were they working on behalf of the police and the fracking industry to minimise protest? By that stage of the campaign, the industry was facing increased resistance wherever they went, so it made sense that they need people to do the undercurrent work. Furthermore, police forces were already underfunded and understaffed, without operating against determined environmentalists day in, day out. At that time, I was still unaware of the link between the Roberts brothers, but in retrospect, with Ian's brother Mark being the lead police officer against fracking protests, it was easy to see why Ian was doing his bidding on behalf of the industry. I say industry, and not just the police, because it was clear to me that if the industry could not use the police's protection services, it could not operate. The two worked hand-in-hand.

Superintendent Dave Hannan, head of specialist operations at North Yorkshire Police, stated that campaigners would be allowed to slow down delivery lorries for only twenty minutes, once in the morning and once in the afternoon. Plus, any demonstrations would take place in only two designated areas. It was also widely claimed that Hannan said these walks would stop if there were any direct-action protests, such as climbing on lorries.

The Frack Free Four are sentenced
In late September, the Frack Free Four, as they were being labelled, went on trial at Preston Crown Court, charged with the criminal offence of 'public nuisance' for their lorry surfing action at the end of the Rolling Resistance at PNR. Julian Brock represented himself in

court earlier, where he pleaded guilty to the offence and was sentenced to twelve months in custody, suspended for eighteen months, so if he didn't commit any crimes in that period, he would not go to prison. I knew all too well from my troubled earlier years that pleading guilty in a criminal court generally leads to a lesser sentence.

The other three activists, who belonged to the quasi-campaign group RTP, had a separate legal team. All pleaded not guilty, but were then of course found guilty. The case was then adjourned for sentencing until the twenty-fifth of September 2018. On the return date, the Judge His Honour Robert Altham, suggested sentencing would be delayed for a further twenty-four hours. This failed not guilty verdict, inevitably leads to a sentence the next level up, in line with court guidelines, so Simon Blevins and Richard Roberts received sixteen months imprisonment, while Loizou received fifteen months. Had Brock not pleaded guilty and stood trial with the other three, and all pleaded not guilty, they all would have all likely received the lesser sentence. But he was pleading according to his own counsel, not wanting to take direction from RTP activists as he knew something was suspicious.

What Brock didn't realise, at the time, was that none of the RTP activists would have been sent to jail. Historical evidence right back to the first Climate Camp in 2006 shows any NGOs connected with Climate Camp never faced jail for their direct actions. When seventeen activists from No Dash for Gas, led by Ewa Jasiewicz, occupied the central cooling tower at the EDF West Burton power plant for a week in October 2012 in a much more dangerous, disruptive and lengthy action, even they didn't go to prison. Of course, there is a difference between peaceful protest and criminal activity, but the justice system sentencing guidelines are there for all to see.

Suppose the action was planned as a diversion from the rig's entrance to the drill site? If so, it was no wonder RTP lawyers were trying to get Brock to plead not guilty, enabling the judicial system to give them all a suspended sentence in line with similar more extreme actions. But Brock, unlike the professional RTP campaigners, wouldn't have been aware of this situation, or how these groups work hand-in-hand with the authorities and legal teams, before he boarded the lorry. In fairness to Brock, I would have taken the same option if faced with prison, because it was hard to get away from the evidence. Also, after witnessing PNR events, I would not have stood in the dock being portrayed as part of RTP.

So, sadly these three innocent activists had now been jailed and all protestors were shocked, fearing this could set a precedent. But of course it didn't (for now), and thankfully, three weeks later, the court of appeal ruled their sentences were inappropriate and freed them with immediate effect. Soon after, the trio walked free from Preston prison, greeted with hugs and cheers from dozens of supporters.

People power at Kirby Misperton
Also in September, the trucks started rolling in to Kirby Misperton, with the required equipment needed for the frack operation. The local community, regular village people, stepped forward and blockaded the site, day after day. They were a fine example of a middle-England community, prepared to be arrested for protecting their environment, whilst eating cake and drinking tea supplied by the ever-resilient, seventy-nine-year-old Jackie Brookes. Many of the protestors were local, including a farmer, university lecturer, a bishop and GPs. These people never imagined they'd be confronting police officers or lying down in front of a truck, but when democracy fails people are left no choice. More than eighty arrests took place between September and October, which included many local people of differing ages.

At the heart of this successful campaign was an occupation on the twenty-first of October. Two men and a woman, climbed the platform sixty-feet high at three o' clock in the morning and stayed there until the next day. The activists claimed that the action was in direct response to Third Energy's announcement it would begin fracking later that week. However, INEOS were attempting to get an industry-wide injunction and this action fell between the September and November hearings. Anyway, soon after, there was a challenge to Greg Clark MP, regarding the finances of Third Energy, which was successful some months later, so thankfully no further work occurred on site.

Twenty-One

The INEOS High Court Ruling

I WAS SIX weeks into my MSc course when I had to head to London again for the three-day hearing on the thirty-first of October. Jon and Val Mager, from the Crawberry Hill campaign, who I trusted and respected, went in my place the first day, as I had a family funeral to attend. I had a debrief with them that evening over dinner, to hear I only missed INEOS's lawyers setting out their exaggerated arguments.

By now, Corre had slightly changed his opinion it 'seemed' on slow-walking protests because he had a deeper understanding of their importance, but it was still left to my legal team to argue for this, as we had approached it in the initial hearing. We made this central to our views because we understood how vital it was. Planning applications were passing all the time at the local level, and when they were not, as in Lancashire, the Communities Minister would overrule at the national government level. Therefore, the only defence communities had left available was to use their bodies to block it, regardless of how much that cost the police force.

During this hearing, it came to light that a meeting took place in London, during May, with the fracking industry, Eclipse strategic security services, the National Police Chiefs Council (NPCC), and the Counter Terrorism Policing National Operations Centre (CTPNOC), no doubt in response to the failed pen at PNR. The

NPCC and CTPNOC advised INEOS that they had enough evidence to obtain an injunction. I was shocked and alarmed because here we had state bodies enabling the destruction of our human rights on behalf of one of the wealthiest companies in Europe. No longer could I be called paranoid; the evidence was clear for all to see that many state bodies were working together to create injunctions stopping protest through the civil courts. And with so many state bodies involved, there had to be intelligence agents and actors at work in the anti-fracking movement, to help steer it their way. No wonder the NGOs were silent.

I now realised that Eclipse, the strategic security services involved, known for their security work against 'insurgents' in the Iraq and Kuwait oil fields, were monitoring anti-fracking activists for the industry. Their office in Herefordshire is also the SAS home, which made sense of the shocking reality of what we had been facing in the previous months and years to protect the environment. I wondered if any of these Eclipse employees were disguised as anti-fracking protestors on and off camp.

Other evidence from the court had shown RTP and Rothery-founded group actions with various different names gave the industry just what they needed to impose injunctions. I had already questioned whether those early May actions by the FFL hierarchy, the Greenpeace action and the Rolling Resistance violence and chaos, were the icing on the cake evidence for the industry. Sadly, I was right. So naturally I wondered whether the NPCC or CTPNOC had been working with agents on the ground to orchestrate and oversee the strategy all along. Did they plan the Rolling Resistance on the back of that May meeting? It was not out of the question after witnessing the orchestrated events before the pen hearing.

At the end of the three-day hearing, Justice Morgan postponed judgement until later in November. Another disappointing delay when we had hoped for a decision.

§

On the twenty-third of November 2017, Justice Morgan gave his ruling and renewed the pre-emptive injunction. This ruling was equal to his previous order, excluding harassment. On this issue, quoted in a Drill or Drop article, Morgan said, "There are likely to be strongly expressed objections to fracking. The expression of those objections may lead to the making of abusive and insulting comments about INEOS (and indeed about the individual Claimants who have made their land available to INEOS) where there might be real difficulty in knowing whether the conduct amounts to harassment. I do not consider that the Claimants have demonstrated a need for the court to make an order against harassment. I consider that such an order could have undesirable consequences which the court would wish to avoid."

What INEOS were trying to obtain was a restraining order from social media attacks against their business.

In granting the injunction related to the supply chain, Morgan accepted the evidence provided by INEOS, saying that they were justified to, "protect people on an around sites and supply chain". On our central issue, slow walking, he held that, "The 'walking' by the protestors was at an unnaturally slow pace... A court would view that standing still to block the passage of vehicles on the highway because the vehicles used for a purpose to which the protestor objects would not be a reasonable use of the highway. I do not see the somewhat token amount of movement involved in slow-walking would change the legal assessment of the protestors' actions. The fracking operators' rights should prevail over the protesters' claims to be entitled to do what they do under Articles 10 and 11. The protestors are doing much more than expressing their opinions about the undesirability of fracking. They are taking direct action against the fracking operators in an attempt to stop their fracking activities. It would not be surprising in such a case that the court would take the view that balancing these entitlements to freedom of expression and assembly against the rights of others, the balance is struck in favour of protecting the rights of others from a direct interference with those rights."

The decision was in line with the ruling in Samede versus City of London. This judgment would now mean individuals would be in contempt of court unless their activities were previously held to be lawful in all circumstances. So, banner waving or managed protest could go ahead, most likely for fifteen minutes, once a week, which Rothery had already agreed with Cuadrilla at PNR. If a person fell foul of a breach and was then arrested, they could face a two-year prison sentence and a £5000 fine.

It was a bitter blow to grassroots protest and success for those who promote NGOs and petition-signing on behalf of the industrial complex, such as Mark Roberts and Rothery herself. As one of many who values their fundamental rights to peaceful political protest, I found this decision profoundly troubling. Although we had minor success in removing the harassment aspect of the order, the rest of the injunction could not be left unchallenged.

At this High Court ruling, I learned how easy it was for anyone to create quasi-experimental, direct-action groups in this new technocratic world. Was Rothery leading an operation to curtail peaceful protest with a mob of people who did not represent me, or anyone else for that matter, apart from prominent climate organisations and government?

In this case, the quasi-group in question was RTP alongside its Occupy associates, who had developed out of another quasi-group, designed from another quasi-group, Climate Camp. Of course, this always has the effect of hiding the overarching group's face, so you never really know who is in charge, or who exactly was involved in taking the focus away from genuinely concerned campaigners and researchers wanting to protect their community.

This decision's magnitude was astounding because we had a situation where anyone who creates online posts with threats of disruption to a company would award that company an injunction. Every unethical business or corporation could now quite easily manipulate the system to gain an injunction against any form of protest, apart from banner waving.

I knew then society was in real trouble. It felt like a corporate takeover of the state, aided by the (non-appearance of) NGOs. Sure enough, not long after, injunctions were granted under similar circumstances for the high-end fashion company Canada Goose on

Regent Street in London using the INEOS case as precedent to stop animal rights activists, aka 'persons unknown', protesting outside their premises. My court system experience now told me this would be the beginning of the floodgates opening for unethical companies outlawing protest and only the Court of Appeal could stop it. So, I filed for appeal.

In the words of my solicitor Rosa Curling: "Free speech is at the heart of any democracy. This case is about the right to protest, a right which has always been, and must continue to be, a fundamental aspect of peaceful political action in our society. Without the right to protest effectively, the ability of citizens to peacefully challenge injustices will be severely curtailed."

§

The trial for my final arrest that summer at Marriott Drilling Company was held in Chesterfield Magistrates Court in December later that year, in front of a District Judge, so I was legally represented by Helen White of Howells. During that trial, myself and another campaigner had no case to answer within minutes of the trial beginning and the other four charged with aggravated trespass were all found not guilty. The judge said he was extremely disappointed that the police failed to investigate the real crime that occurred that day, a security guard using his vehicle as a weapon and endangering life. Justice served once again. Again, we celebrated justice being served, with the local community.

That was the end of my anti-fracking arrests, which consisted of being bailed away from four different counties Humberside, Greater Manchester, North East Derbyshire and Lancashire, over the course of three years, denying me the right to exercise my rights to protest.

Twenty-Two

Protection of Rothery Runs Deep

EARLY 2018 BEGAN with my legal team and I, plus Corre and his lawyers, having a meeting at Matrix Chambers in London to explore how environmental lawyers might assist further in the case, if we were to obtain an appeal. Ten of us sat around the table, including the top human rights lawyers supporting my case, but not Corre. Ten minutes in and Corre arrives. Pretty soon he starts talking in a roundabout way about me stepping aside from the case. *What? Was he seriously proposing I leave it all to him?* If I dropped out, there would be no opposition to slow walking; because that was not part of his case in the High Court, therefore he was unable to appeal on those grounds. Without me fighting for it, there would also be no objection to demonstrating at any businesses along the supply chain of the oil and gas industry. That only left the 'persons unknown' aspect.

Had Corre forgotten one vital issue? There are criminal courts for criminality, which is the right course of action where justice should be heard, not in a civil court, for direct action. There was no need for injunctive relief for INEOS in the first place, because they had the criminal courts for unlawful activity against their business, if and when it occurred. It was clear, though, Corre was dividing protest tactics, and trying to stop my chance of rightfully opposing this injunction, representing everyone's right to protest in any lawful way they deem necessary, not just managed, polite, mostly ineffective protest. I was astounded. But I stayed quiet, listening to make sure I was hearing him right. *He's a smart man,* I thought to myself, *who is giving him such bad advice?* When that hour and a half meeting finished, my legal team and I were not happy. We decided to distance ourselves more from Corre and his team going forward. Our sides to the case were different anyway, I represented Articles 10 and 11 of the ECHR, and him law-abiding citizens. If Corre and his legal team had their way, only banner waving and petition signing would have been the future, in line with the government's wishes, and not going to stop the onshore oil and gas industry, or any other unethical business for that matter. The only way to stop it was to blockade it in person, and I fully intended to fight for the right to do just that. Nevertheless, it wasn't going to affect climate NGOs, Greenpeace had proved that at PNR. Strangely, when the meeting ended, Corre barely said a word to me and left. Then I was sure he was getting bad advice. Curiously, he had also recruited Claire Stephenson of FFL, as a media admin who dutifully reported his involvement in the legal challenge but neglected to do so with mine.

Tactics in Lancashire get nastier

At Kirby Misperton fracking site, a sign now read, "Closing down sale, everything must go!" You had to love the anti-fracking community's creativity, a community that, not long after, witnessed the fracking equipment's beautiful vacation of their area. Here, a non-negotiable community said no, and meant no, unlike a minority in Lancashire claiming to represent the majority, claiming to say no, whilst facilitating the industry and police to limit protest. It was another example of how grassroots community activism is critical to a functioning democracy, rather than relying on NGOs, who are barely there, then turn up for a week, cause chaos, then depart. The bibs and headscarves of the Yorkshire Nanas are now in storage, washed and ready for their next outing, should they be required.

For the next six months, I continued with my MSc studies, only contributing online but still following the campaign intensely.

During this period, such was the vitriol being whipped up against anyone that didn't fall into line, one local campaigner to the PNR site shockingly had a rag and matches put through his letterbox, which thankfully didn't catch alight while he was sleeping. Geza Frackman called for a day of truce at Maple Farm, which he named 'High Noon'. However, when he arrived, he was confronted by Dunne, Brown, Hobson, Yellowbelly, Danby, and McCann who set out to agitate him for a reaction. It was all set up before he turned up, with the police waiting in the wings to arrest Geza for an assault that never occurred, with Brown and McCann doing the work of the Forward Intelligence Team thrusting their cameras in Frackman's face.

I watched the livestream from home and was disgusted by how these people were operating. Rothery and Stephenson were seen jumping up and down for joy and hugging each other openly declaring their delight at Geza's wrongful arrest. A small group of locals who witnessed the blatant lies and obvious set up that led to an innocent man being arrested went to the station to offer him support when he was released. This was enough to make each one of them the subjects of further bullying, intimidation, lies, smears and exclusion from groups, all from members of FFL, McCann and O'Connor. You might expect such abuse from industry but these people were allegedly anti-frackers and supposed to be on the same side. The fact that one of the bullied and slandered was a child, Morgan Marshall, just fifteen at the time, didn't make him off limits either. This tactical approach was psychological abuse in pack mentality and all very professional.

After this event, what happened in the long months ahead in Little Plumpton was a war on people's psychology that concluded with not one person standing outside gates on many days. Of course, Rothery was still telling the world she was blocking the industry day in day out and the Guardian was foolishly reporting it. Or were they also gaslighting the general public? It wouldn't be the first time.

The majority of the original 2014 Lancashire Nanas, and more, had come and gone after abuse and attacks from Rothery and Daniels for not towing their line. Rothery's lack of resistance to Cuadrilla was very noticeable to anyone brave enough to speak out. Only those involved with the hierarchy of FFL, and those who could be easily manipulated now remained, the majority of which were well-meaning but duped pensioners. Rothery needed people to film her and follow her or she was redundant. So basically, if you were willing to dress up in what ever colour or costume you were told and parade in an entourage behind her, you were in.

In April 2018, a direct action took place involving an original Lancashire Nana, Diane Steels, who was a stalwart at Barton Moss. She said: "It was nearly four years after Barton Moss and I felt frustrated we weren't having more effect at PNR. I realised a bit too late that being part of the Nanas came at a price. I didn't want to be controlled or be part of any deal-making with the frackers. All our plans for action were 'leaked' to social media in advance, making our actions pointless. When news of the deal with Tina and the frackers erupted on social media in January 2017, locals became angry and felt betrayed. I didn't blame them, I felt the same. All we worked so hard for was going down the pan. I wanted to know the truth about it and asked on the Nana Facebook Group, only to be told how dare I question Tina."

Steels continued, "No fuss, no announcement, I along with a few other Nanas detached ourselves to do our own thing. I knew I had to do direct action myself, and not staged for the media. I contacted someone I trusted to arrange it. The day before it was supposed to happen our lock-on device mysteriously went missing. Someone must have got wind somehow. I was fuming, then realised it was because direct action was forbidden on a Wednesday because the Women in White had an arrangement with police and frackers to do their protest. Tina had said the Women in White was nothing to do with fracking though." So what was it about?

Steels continued, "I was determined, so it was rearranged for the following week. Only a few people knew in advance. It went perfectly, four of us locked on to two devices. Unlike other actions we had very little support. No appearance from the Nanas or the usual crowd of anti-fracking activists. There was support from lovely locals who certainly weren't expecting to see me locked on. I didn't care about little support, I just did the action, got arrested and received my trophy spork (a spork is what is given with food at the police station, a memento for environmental activists)".

Centralisation and the collapse of the campaign

Rothery created yet another new quasi-group that April, called United Resistance (I had lost cost count by now, too). Months earlier, during the Kirby Misperton campaign, a Ryedale campaigner also wanting to be a politician, Steve Mason, had established a centralised organisation called Frack Free United. Rothery was the face on the ground, Steve Mason controlled the media through Frack Free United. Both were attempting to further their careers and standings whilst centralising the movement. And both were also making it more and more about climate change rather than protecting communities against specific toxic industries, by being the indirect voice of groups, even if many of those group members never completely agreed with his message.

I felt that neither Rothery nor Mason had done much more than raise the fracking industry profile without really getting in its way. Rothery, the self-proclaimed leader of the anti-fracking movement and Lancashire campaign, did not even speak during Lancashire County Council's planning decision or subsequent Appeal. However, both were discursive, controlling all narratives within the drive to make sure specific individuals could have a voice whilst silencing the broader activist community; it was a full-on attempt of a centralised campaign, which we had fought hard against throughout.

However, local campaigners on the ground knew it was all about control as there had been little unity nationally for almost three years. The evidence of previous successes was the result of other communities taking a decentralised approach against the industry enemy on the ground and in the courts. A centralised system was essential to the frackers and police, as the great man who was Ian Crane knew very well, having lived and breathed the protest on the ground at Barton Moss, Kirby Misperton and Crawberry Hill. Was this why the climate change brigade was keen to label him as divisive, to gaslight his opposition to their centralisation tactics?

To me, Crane was more about unity – in stopping the fracking industry get a foothold in our land. He was all for communities deciding for themselves and was always approachable to anyone who wanted to ask him any questions. Like me, Crane saw a centralised approach as a perfect weapon to destroy the movement because specific individuals would take the lead, and we had already witnessed these individuals' destructive discourse. This centralisation was dangerous to the campaign because those proclaiming to be leaders would control every section of the movement. But we were not intending to let this happen.

The NGOs played their part in disinformation after their silence around the injunction. In March, Greenpeace angered me and many others in the anti-fracking movement in Lancashire after promoting Rothery in the world's top five-badass women. Of course, Rothery was still promoting herself as Blackpool's saviour whilst continuing her weekly worship of Cuadrilla with the Women in White. I am not sure whether the protest was a symbol of surrender or to do with race because of the absence of people from more racially mixed backgrounds. It may have been touted as a peaceful presence of women at the roadside near the site but what good would it do? It wasn't stopping the industry one bit, and was exclusive on gender and, by observation, ethnicity lines.

Many campaigners thought it was embarrassing and were angered by the sight of the police marching down the duel carriage way, stopping the traffic and annoying people, all to facilitate Rothery's twenty minutes of ego stroking every week. They knew full well, that anyone else on the road at any other time, trying to do something to actually hinder the frackers, would be arrested and risk getting a criminal record. If ever there was a time to knock it on the head it was when all other forms of protest were prohibited, but the woman has no shame. This arrogance betrayed her though, because even some of those who had participated in her theatrics previously could see that an arranged and agreed protest for twenty minutes one day a week was no protest at all and not the behaviour you would expect from a self-proclaimed leader of the anti-fracking movement.

The local activists built another tower at the bellmouth entrance to the site, at four o' clock in the morning on the twenty-seventh of May 2018. It was the sixteenth birthday of Morgan, the son of local campaigners Sue and Richard Marshall, and they supplied a running buffet of sandwiches and cake for people who came. They advertised the party but not the tower in the hope to get numbers. The person delivering the buffet got threatened with a fine for simply pulling up in the police welfare space that Rothery and Daniels always parked in. Only those involved knew about it at first but significantly, the Rothery crew never supported their call to fill the bellmouth and support the action.

The Police Chief Inspector Ogle was called off the golf course to assess the situation. This pleased the locals greatly as he turned up in his shorts and t-shirt which indicated to them that the police hadn't been expecting it. Those who would usually turn up to support Rothery's parties and photo shoots were all absent and remained silent, and Maple India Media's John O'Connor, only came at the end of the second day to film the destruction of the tower and mock that it hadn't lasted long. It was obvious by now, Maple Indie Media was formed by McCann and O'Connor in 2017 to promote the narrative required by the FFL hierarchy.

These locals put a call out for solidarity all day Monday to help fill the bellmouth as they had stopped the fuel tanker getting in and knew it would be back first thing Tuesday. Sure enough, it was, and they managed to prevent it getting in when three locals created a disturbance further up the road. This only left two people sitting next to the tower as the police started to cordon it off. If the Rothery crew had supported the tower, they could have helped delay the police dismantling it and cutting out the two people inside. So not really the resistance to Cuadrilla or climate change that one might have expected, in this instance.

Rothery soon created yet another quasi-group, claiming to be the new suffragettes, an absolute disgrace considering what those brave women had to go through to get the vote, without doing protest deals. I guess images of women dressed as suffragettes in Parliament Square got the photos to attract the attention, but again, it wasn't going to stop any drilling operation. Plus, by now, all the messaging was the over-arching climate change zeal rather than community-based environment protection.

In October, her veil finally slipped off to reveal the real nastiness behind the mask at the Conservative Party conference in Birmingham. At the conference with the quasi-suffragettes, Rothery filmed herself rowing with Miriam Lewis, the ex-partner of Sir Lindsey Hoyle, the Speaker of the House of Commons. Lewis was on her way to speak at a fringe meeting on domestic abuse and how she believed her daughter's relationship had affected her state of mind before her death in December 2017. In the video, Lewis engaged with campaigners until she faced Rothery, who challenged her, in her usual concerned grandmother discourse with added verbal abuse. It was very unlike Rothery in front of the camera, but I guess everyone has a day off when they live a lie.

Chorley MP Sir Lindsay Hoyle said: "There was simply no justification for the cruel and undignified comments reportedly made by this campaigner."

The understanding of how the Green movement protects Rothery came from the Green Party itself, saying, "The Green Party does not condone these comments, and we acknowledge that a full apology has been made. No further action is currently being taken." Hardly surprising, when Rothery had only been promoted the previous October to one of its eight national committees, the campaigns committee.

So Greenpeace claimed she was one of the top five-badass women globally, and the Green Party promoted her to their Campaigns Committee, all while she was working with Lancashire Police, destroying anti-fracking movement unity and helping the state limit protest. Those who supported Rothery could not countenance that she was, in fact, working with the police. After all, she was still being supported by NETPOL in March 2019, who had the audacity to use a clip of me in a video of me educating the police on the dangers of fracking outside Preston County Hall, four years earlier, under the headline, 'Do not speak to the police'. I realised later, the video was made by Gathering Place Films' Nina Tailor, a close ally of Rothery, so I was deeply disturbed with her involvement with NETPOL. This stunt was unsurprising because Tailor could have used one of a great many pictures of Rothery standing talking to PLOs at PNR and even giving flowers to one police officer in some quasi-ceremony at the gates of the site. But then, she most definitely did speak to the police in order to do their bidding and control protest. So why did Tailor leave Rothery out of that video?

Twenty-Three

More Corruption Revealed and Cuadrilla Gathers Evidence

REMEMBER, AMANDA WEBSTER the protest buster? Well, her links to those at the top of the Frack Free Lancashire hierarchical structure were now being revealed. In 2018, Maureen Mills (Frack Free Lancashire Treasurer) had a garden party at her house in Halsall in Lancashire. One of the attendees on her guest list was the Labour Party's Lancashire's Police and Crime Commissioner Clive Grunshaw, directly involved with the Lancashire Constabulary's Operation Manilla, overseeing policing of the protests.

From being a frontline protestor, I, and others, were becoming professional private investigators on behalf of the national anti-fracking campaign and civil and human rights for just about every other protest group on the planet. I'd certainly been using my spare time between studying and waiting for appeal constructively.

After further research, we discovered that Grunshaw's assistant was none other than the infamous protest buster herself, who was now Deputy District Judge and commercial law consultant, with experience as a Judge in the civil courts. Was this how and why the protest was controlled right from the get-go at PNR? Did Webster provide injunction advice? Did she have input on which case was in the public interest and which was not? Was she advising Mark

Roberts on the policing of anti-fracking protests? Did she have any involvement in 'flare gate' at Barton Moss? So many questions arose from these findings.

Since 2016, Mills herself had been a Labour councillor and spent several years on the planning committees. However, she had failed to declare her interests in several organisations and NGOs until 2018, in particular concerning her husband, a manager for offshore oil and gas. So it was probable that Mills knew Webster, but she certainly knew Grunshaw and Mark Roberts, Regional Lead on Public Order Policing. Then we had the Roberts brothers connection with Julie Daniels, Rothery's sister, who was best of friends with Ian Roberts. Brown, of course, is Rothery's right arm man, and he had the expertise of being a camp member plus Stephenson on media duties. So all angles were covered. Was Rothery's role amongst this pile of professionals purely an attempt to lead the anti-movement on someone's behalf? The plot was thickening all the time.

It was no wonder people were getting acquitted in court on the same charge as others found guilty. Similar cases were not even getting to court because they were not in the public interest. Anyone who understands protest movements knows undercover police or police informants have cases collapsed for precisely this reason. It happened with demonstrations at Gleneagles G8 and Ratcliffe-on-Soar power station, to name just two, when activists weren't even arrested or if they were, their trials collapsed because of the involvement of undercover police. In the case of the Ratcliffe demo, the undercover officer was Mark Stone, better known as PC Mark Kennedy, the now-exposed undercover police officer who spent seven years infiltrating a group of environmental activists.

The controlled NGO environmental movement, stemming at least from Climate Camp, has most likely been infiltrated for decades. Collectively, many organisations were working together from the top down to deny any grassroots protest unless they controlled it, to save a police budget, no matter whether they fracked or not. Were any of them even concerned about fracking, but rather intent on eradicating the rights to protest? I was questioning everything I'd witnessed now. Was the taking of the field in 2014 planned with authorities beforehand? I was beginning to believe it was. It would have saved Cuadrilla costs on security and costs to the police. Was the Rothery £55,000 case pre-planned ahead with the authorities? It certainly had the success of giving her a high-profile position before her deceitful role, just weeks before Cuadrilla started work. Did Rothery create a deal with industry and police for only thirteen people to protest? Certainly, otherwise why would she have been promoting it?

Greenpeace was right to declare Rothery a badass; she denied the community their rights to protest. A masterstroke of gaslighting by Greenpeace on all accounts, with a hint of satirical satanism. However, that was not the end of it. This dangerous pantomime to abolish all protest (not just anti-fracking), unless managed, was like an out-of-control juggernaut.

Block Around the Clock creates the evidence
In July 2018, with Cuadrilla's injunction still active but soon to expire, and the High Court precedent from the INEOS case now in full force, Cuadrilla still needed a plan after Alan MacClean QC, on behalf of INEOS, had failed to extend the injunction to represent the whole industry. Therefore, a program required creating to strengthen Rothery's, Lancashire Constabulary's and Cuadrilla's control of the protest outside the PNR site, after their attempt to put protestors in a pen failed. Mark Roberts had now taken a new role with South Yorkshire Police and the NPCC, so his involvement is unknown.

Of course, they would need to work with their trusted colleagues within RTP to succeed. This strategic plan with RTP took place during the Rothery-led three month discursive banner of United Resistance against Cuadrilla. The central part would be the RTP Block Around the Clock event, as part of their Break the Chain campaign, posted on social media. The Block Around the Clock event was weeks away, so Cuadrilla used the event page on Facebook as evidence. This event page by RTP would establish the 'real and imminent threat' of interruption to their business, which Cuadrilla would now allegedly be facing, now easily proved to be in line with the previous INEOS ruling.

If these people weren't working with Cuadrilla, the event page itself, would give Cuadrilla the time to reschedule in advance, so no 'real and inminent threat'. For example, Cuadrilla would just rearrange any site deliveries to other days, so there would be no block on them at all, just as there was no blockade for the rig. There would have been a slight inconvenience for site workers, but in the long game of controlling the protest, which was now years in, that inconvenience would be minimal. As predicted, Cuadrilla applied to the courts to vary their previous injunction, which was still valid, but this time they wanted a stretch of pavements and highway (public land) outlawed from any protests outside the site. It would be the final nail in the coffin of protesting on public land without authorities' consent outside the Cuadrilla site, with it the end of Rothery and Daniels services. But would that event page be enough evidence to obtain the injunction?

During the United Resistance, because of the devastation certain agents had on the protest, arrests had significantly dropped compared to the same time in 2017. Therefore, it was debatable whether the Judge would agree on a 'real and imminent threat' on the RTP Facebook event alone. As a guarantee, Rothery, Daniels and others who had supported them throughout, saw fit to to create a discursive action to give Cuadrilla's lawyers all the evidence they needed of increasing arrests: the Caravan of Love.

On the twenty-second of May 2018, the day after Cuadrilla issued papers for an injunction, a caravan was towed and placed outside gates of the drilling site. Over the next forty hours, twelve people locked on, all involved being used by Rothery and Daniels to create the further evidence needed for the next injunction. Incredibly, Rothery was involved in this action, although she never lasted forty hours, just after midnight on the first night she swapped her place with someone else. Eventually, everyone else was cut out and arrested, charged with willful obstruction of the highway.

Juggling university and campaigning

Still hard at work on my Masters course, I decided my dissertation would be in the area of environmental health rather than addiction, as first intended. A pharmacologist PhD student at my University was doing her doctoral thesis on schoolchildren's exercise level, comparing a cohort in a smoking household to one that was smoke-free. I saw the opportunity there for me to measure air pollution at primary schools, so she could also use some of this data. With my International Studies degree and activism, again I was the right person in the right place at the right time, so I set out to create a research proposal for my dissertation.

My study was a quantitative assessment of temporal and spatial concentration levels of air pollution (particle matter) PM2.5 indoors and outdoors in the school microenvironment. I would attend ten different primary schools, once a week, and measure the air quality on the roads around the school and the playground, between eight-thirty and nine-fifteen in the morning. I would then leave an air quality monitor inside the school to observe various levels on seven successive days. The study also involved me using GPS to track my position to time and place, which I correlated with PM2.5 data to visually show the reader's hotspot times and locations. It was fascinating to undertake. Five years earlier, I could not have envisaged writing a quantitative masters dissertation such as this.

I was so pleased to achieve a first-class mark on my dissertation, one of the best for the year. I had spent sometimes over twenty-four hours a day in the library, analysing my data and writing up, so consequently I'd not had that much time for activism. But I still managed to print about 10,000 copies of documents and reports for the upcoming Cuadrilla case, which Ian Crane, Benjamin Dean, Bob Dennett and Sharon Whale were working on putting together to challenge. By now, multi-tasking university and the campaign was standard, so I just used the time to stretch myself further.

Incredibly, but unsurprisingly, all the NGOs were still silent, including FoE, Greenpeace and of course, FFL. But then, we had already witnessed firsthand all of the forenamed groups' non-representation in the High Court in 2014, 2016 and 2017. They were clearly not at all interested or bothered.

On the day of the Cuadrilla injunction hearing, on the eleventh of July 2018, Rothery was outside with a crowd. All the usual climate change campaigners and an updated collection of nanas were there speaking to the media, even including the BBC, as if Rothery supported us inside fighting for the people of Lancashire, and all campaigners everywhere. Of course, Rothery couldn't care less: a year earlier had even said, "What the fuck are they doing here?" outside the same court under similar circumstances at the failed sheep pen hearing. There she'd had no entourage or even press, as she meant that day to be quiet before and after. Now I knew why: it was the first legal move to comply with industry and police to bring in managed protest, so she wouldn't have wanted witnesses.

Today, she knew, as we did, that we could not win because the previous High Court judgement of the INEOS injunction had proven there was a 'real and imminent threat'. Yet there she was manipulating the watching public like she had so many times before. Such carefully managed, manipulative stunts made me question how much the media were involved in this corruption too. It was already evident that she had special treatment with the mainstream local media sources in Blackpool and Judy Hobson of the BBC. The majority of any mainstream media articles and NGO reports on the Women in White or the Lancashire Nanas are mostly all about Rothery and how she resisted Cuadrilla. Plus, from the beginning of her involvement she was able to speak incredibly well and clearly about the climate change issue, in particular, especially for a novice grandmother campaigner. It was almost as if she was professionally trained.

Inevitably, we were unsuccessful at the hearing. and Judge Pelling QC, as predicted, claimed there was an 'real and imminent threat', from RTP, whom of course Rothery had worked hand-in-hand with in anti-fracking since 2013. Paragraph sixteen of his judgement said, "The evidence suggests that many of those responsible for unlawful activity have been encouraged to attend at the site and to participate in such unlawful activity by a group calling itself Reclaim the Power. However, that group is difficult to identify, as are its individual members."

The Judge continued in paragraph fifty-five, "I consider the requirements, therefore, before an injunction of this sort can be granted, to be satisfied, particularly given the contents of the Reclaim the Power press release referred to earlier."

During the hearing, Cuadrilla used photos and videos of Rothery's Caravan of Love action, which conveniently happened at exactly the right time for them to add this evidence to their court bundle. A table of arrests from the previous months was used to show one part of a real and imminent threat, with this action helping to make it look as though arrests were on the increase, as in 2017.

Although, we knew we would fail at the hearing, we had to challenge this, because the case would be open to challenge if I was successful in the INEOS Court of Appeal hearing. A strange and significant omission from this injunction was the once-a-week, hour-long, lunchtime Women in White event.

Paragraph forty-five of the judgement said, "In the course of submissions made by the individual defendants, they drew attention to a weekly march by local protesters styled "Women in White". It was submitted, and not disputed by the claimants (Cuadrilla), that this weekly march was conducted at a time and on a day agreed informally with the local police. It is accepted by the claimants that this should be an 'exception' created to permit protest activity to occur, and the order now reflects that."

So there you have it, the only protest allowed at PNR now was to be a once-a-week event as agreed with the police. And that wasn't going to stop the frackers, or slow them down.

That was the end of anti-fracking direct action protests at PNR for the most part; the agencies had done their job in eradicating any. I said at the time that the Caravan of Love case would not get to court, it would either run out of time, or the CPS would drop it. I was correct, and two years later, in June 2020, the CPS said, "The decision to discontinue these charges has been taken because a prosecution is not needed in the public interest". I would go as far as to say it was in the public's interest, but not in the authorities' interest.

Twenty-Four

The Court of Appeal Hearing and Decision

IN THE WEEKS leading up to my Court of Appeal hearing in Spring 2019, overwhelmed by the appeal's pressure and the ongoing psychological abuse from these professional gaslighters, I had a short relapse in my recovery from gambling. I could generally get to around twelve months gamble free, and then this would happen. Although I was continually risking my recovery, I had to keep going because I had come this far and too much was at stake. I could fight that personal battle another day. Thankfully, I still had my support group at Gamblers Anonymous and I needed them now more than ever. So I attended some meetings and had some conversations with people at GA who had known me from the start of my recovery. They mentored me through this turbulent and stressful time, and helped me get back on track.

In the days leading up to the appeal, I went shopping for a sharp suit to make sure I was representing professionally. I could have turned up in camp clothes, but, after all, I was representing the people at the Court of Appeal. It's the right thing to do, isn't it? Certainly, for scousers!

The Court of Appeal on the Strand in London had always been a building of importance to me. I knew, if we were ever to be successful in this case, it would be in this building. Some people say all courts are corrupt, but that has never been how I have seen them. Justice is for everyone when it affects human rights, and this case involved everyone, no matter how wealthy or poor. This was not a Magistrate's Court or High Court in the civil division, human rights Judges sit on those benches. Although we still had Supreme Court and Strasbourg options, they would be a way off; and in that time, any other industry would be free to charge right through communities.

Close to the appeal date, FoE wanted to put a written submission in, which I reluctantly accepted (Lord Justices may have allowed it anyway), after their total absence. No doubt they were wishing to look credible to grassroots campaigners, who were by now questioning what they actually did. On the fifth and sixth of March 2019, some sixteen months after the November 2017 judgement, our appeal took place. It was an exhausting two days, where my legal team put forward compelling arguments. Afterwards, I was hopeful of justice because the three Lord Justice's presiding over the appeal asked tough questions over INEOS's claims. However, you can never be sure until the eventual handing down of the decision, which the Lord Justices reserved judgement on until a later date. Yet more waiting.

Celebrating the win

Four weeks later, on the third of April 2019, in a reserved judgement, Lord Justice Longmore, Lord Justice David Richards and Lord Justice Leggatt ruled that sections of the injunction were, indeed, unlawful. I already knew the decision a week before because the legal team showed me a copy of the draft, in confidence. I could not disclose its contents to any other person, in the public domain, or take any course of action in response to the judgement before the Lord Justices themselves handed it down or I could face twelve months in prison. It was the longest week of my life because I wanted to tell everyone and celebrate.

My legal team could not make the hand down at the Court because they were dealing with another case, so I didn't travel down to London for it. But I found out that in the trespass part of the injunction, there was no appropriate time limit, so the Lord Justices remitted this back to the High Court, having accepted my teams' arguments. The argument was that the High Court had failed to consider the test for the granting of interim injunctions in cases restricting the right to free speech. This case is still to be heard, now over two years later.

Furthermore, the Lord Justices struck out the other injunctions entirely, because the High Court had failed to properly balance everyone's right to protest against INEOS' commercial interests. Lord Justice Longmore highlighted the potentially chilling effects of the requests on lawful protest, saying, "The citizen's right of protest is not to be diminished by advance fear of committal except in the clearest of cases."

About the central objection of my arguments on the eradication of slow walking, Longmore said, "The concept of slow walking in front of vehicles or, more generally, obstructing the highway may not result in any damage to the claimants at all." He questioned, "How slow is slow? Any speed slower than a normal walking speed of two miles per hour? One does not know," concluding that, "A person faced with such an injunction may well be chilled into not obstructing the highway at all." In doing so, the case is now lead judgement in England and Wales on such cases involving protests and injunctions.

At last, after over two years fighting to save our right to protest, we finally had justice restored. Corre, of course, was at the hand down. I spent the day in Chester with Ben and Sharon, who I helped with the pen case, and celebrated the verdict on livestream with champagne on ice. Oh boy, did we celebrate. The FFL hierarchy made a point of my absence in London, no doubt wounded with the decision, which made the celebrations even more satisfying. Corre phoned and correctly pointed out that I was right all along about slow-walking. I did several livestreams, telling certain people what I thought of them, which didn't go down well with some. However, under the extreme pressures and psychological abuse I had received, my outbursts were long overdue. The following weekend, I then celebrated with some of the Lancashire campaigners, in Lancashire, which didn't go down well, with the FFL hierarchy.

FoE claimed the victory was generally theirs, and never even got in touch with a personal message. I wasn't surprised by this because they had never been supportive of our grassroots protest or direct action in all my years in the campaign; this includes their directors from all over the UK turning their backs on Barton Moss activists in 2014. Their in-house lawyer, Katie de Kauwe, said, "This is a massive victory for civil liberties and human rights across the country... Friends of the Earth is proud to be part of this legal action." They were in a win-win situation by joining the proceedings at the final stage. Dave Timms, head of Political Affairs at FoE, said the ruling confirmed their view that the granted INEOS' injunction wrongly and unlawfully stifled protest. Of course, both of them were correct in their statements, but where had they been in the previous years? If they both agreed the injunction was an attack on civil liberties, why was I left to oppose this critical case on my own? I just put it down to FoE having no backbone, the same as they had shown at Barton Moss. However, although I am critical of them, I will say they put every other NGO to shame, none more so than Greenpeace and Liberty.

How do NGOs get the praise on the back of others' work? Are they warned off initially and then see the opportunity to gather some funding, plus make the wider public believe they are doing something? Or are some NGOs even involved in the denial of human rights to protest? After the success of myself and the team involved in the Court of Appeal, FoE then stepped in and took control of altering the Cuadrilla judgement using the INEOS case law. The decision now meant all injunctions granted would be successful under appeal, including oil and gas companies and the Canada Goose case. Strangely, however, the Weald Action Group in the Southern England are continuing their challenge to UKOG at a trial in Spring 2021.

Twenty-Five

Rebellion for Protest Extinction?

THE STRUGGLE TO protect our rights to protest continued, as it always will. Indeed, all the work by agents/actors was not going to end after our success in the Court of Appeal. I had suspected not long after the initial INEOS hearing, in September 2017, the Conservative Government was avoiding changing protest laws through Acts of Parliament. That path would be seen as authoritarian whereas the civil route would disguise that but still protect controversial businesses. Furthermore, within a neoliberal economic system, businesses are largely self-regulating with the state playing a hands-off approach, leaving it up to businesses to protect themselves so the government doesn't interfere with the public's rights.

But remember it was the NPCC and CTPNOC who advised INEOS in May 2017 that they had enough evidence to obtain a wide-ranging injunction - both organisations are connected to the Home Office. Now that the people had been successful at the Court of Appeal, this government-preferred civil route to protect their business interests was exhausted. Therefore, with ever-increasing power transferred to corporations, signatories to climate change treaties requiring social change rather than the system change, there was a problem, which needed a reaction for the solution - the Acts of Parliament. Change of laws in government generally need the legitimacy of the people, and large-scale disruption makes that decision easier to make. It is rarely small protests that bring in new laws, civil or state-led; whether peaceful or not, it is large-scale ones that lead to that kind of change. As I witnessed, with the Cuadrilla and INEOS injunctions, large numbers were seen in evidence to the courts with most of that coming from the quasi-campaign group RTP in conjunction with Occupy personnel.

Step forward Extinction Rebellion (XR), founded in the UK the same month I was granted my right to appeal the INEOS case in May 2018. Now, just twelve days after our successful Court of Appeal judgement, XR were about to begin ten days of widespread disruption in London. The Easter holidays, in April 2019 saw prolonged protests in different areas of Central London: Oxford Circus, Waterloo Bridge, Parliament Square and Marble Arch. The group were saying the government was not listening about climate change and XR had certain demands: that the Government tell the truth about the climate emergency; that the Government must act now to halt biodiversity loss and reduce greenhouse gas emissions by 2025; and that it must be led by a Citizen's Assembly on climate and ecological justice.

I had already seen consensus meetings be steered a certain way by actors/agents in groups. I'm not sure this is any more democratic that the system we have already. Plus, it seemed that XR were sharing a supremely scare-mongering message about the threat of climate change – giving us just over a decade before all humans are wiped out – while not actually protecting the environment from destruction or getting in the way of the worst offending industries right now. So what was the objective of all the disruption? And why right now?

As I watched it all unfold, I saw striking similarities with what was happening in London with the attempted centralisation of anti-fracking protest tactics, which was not surprising, given how many RTP, Climate Camp and Occupy actors/agents are involved in XR. The leaders of Extinction Rebellion agreed on a designated protest location with the Metropolitan Police, at Marble Arch, just as they had done with Occupy in 2011, and as Rothery (a leading figure within XR hierarchy) had done with Lancashire constabulary at

PNR. This was evident by arrests made under S14 of the Public Order Act (yes, that again), which did *not* apply at Marble Arch and where the police encouraged people to head. If Marble Arch was under S14, there would have been a time scale on end of gathering and police would not have sent protestors there.

Leading campaigners in charge at Marble Arch, where the protest was centralised from, were what I and many others call the 'controlled opposition'. Nearly all governments in history have employed this technique of controlled opposition. In the words of Lenin, 'the best way to control the opposition is lead it ourselves'. Those at Marble Arch did not consist of the vast majority, if any, of the grassroots XR campaigners, very much like Maple Farm at PNR. I suspect it had to be this way, so the police had easy access to the leaders and change agents without the majority of XR realising the group is non-horizontal. Therefore, you could only stay in the Marble Arch community if part of their more extensive discursive plan, as this was the data-collecting HQ.

From there, the agents went out, set the scenes, filmed the narrative, whilst in constant contact with the Met and Intelligence Services. These actors/agents are highly trained in evidence gathering and promoting discursive agendas. Some of them can be identified together for over a decade. Several people whom I saw multiple times with expensive video equipment on Geza Frackman's livestreams at Marble Arch, were involved in the intimidation and bullying of anti-fracking campaigners in Lancashire and national activists online, including Hamish Haynes, Maple Indie Media's Fargo McCann and John O'Connor. Other members of Occupy and RTP were regularly seen at this location too.

The other three locations - Oxford Circus, Waterloo Bridge and Occupy's favourite place for case law, Parliament Square - were not publicly agreed, even though XR had widely publicised they would 'Block Around the Clock' at these locations, six days before the events began. Funny they used the same name of the RTP event at PNR, that gave Cuadrilla the clear evidence of a 'real and imminent threat' for its injunction, less than twelve months earlier. But then, it's the same agents/actors in charge. Would the City of London have applied for an injunction against XR protests for a 'real and imminent threat', if I was unsuccessful at Court of Appeal weeks earlier? From what I had witnessed and evidenced in previous years, I very much suspect so, and the Occupy, RTP and XR leaders knew it, which is why they promoted the event a week early to give the City of London lawyers the time to apply to the High Court. Therefore, quite possibly, it would have been the first attempt at a city-wide protest injunction.

Although, the other three locations were not agreed publicly with the Met, they and intelligence services knew there would be large numbers at each location, in advance. So, it was a pretty lame excuse from the Met Police Commissioner Cressida Dick to claim the Met were caught out. It was obvious there would be a massive turnout. After all, Greta Thunberg had been leading the large worldwide student strikes and climate change marches since August 2018. Where the Met actually caught out by the earlier Court of Appeal decision?

The other important issue was that parliament was away for the Easter holidays, so the media had a window for full-scale broadcast, perfect timing for both climate change coverage, protest disruption or, if I'd be been unsuccessful, a widely-publicised step into an Orwellian future of protest eradication. I say perfect timing for coverage on the basis of the statement made by Gail Bradbrook, a leader of XR, whilst standing amidst demonstrators on Waterloo Bridge. She told a Sky News presenter when interviewed, that, "the politicians behind the scenes, including this current government, are telling us that they need a social movement like ours to give them the social permission to do the necessary." The presenter questioning Bradbrook then asked if that really could be the case that the government want XR's help, to which she replied, "I'm giving you anecdotal evidence, I won't be able to prove that to you, but I've met a couple of people who talked to Theresa May's (UK Prime Minister at the time) advisors and they have said they 'do know how bad it is (climate change) and actually they do need you guys to help."

What does she mean? Help do what exactly? Social policy change or the eradication of protest? Or both? Restrict everyone's right to protest, whilst draconian laws are forced on us, with no avenue for recourse? Whatever the answer may be the word 'environmental' has changed to 'social', as the leading narrative on climate change and XR. So there it was, XR, Occupy and RTP are social change groups not an environmental movement. No wonder these agents had been restricting our right to protest the destruction of the environment.

Was one of these ministers talking to Bradbrook behind the scenes Claire Perry, who gave the green light for fracking at PNR? Perry had met members of XR at a summit in Poland in November 2018, and said afterwards, "We had a good and productive chat and have been in correspondence since." Discussions with ministers is hardly the system change they proclaim to want to achieve. But it is not system change that XR is about, it's about social change, bringing about a change in the way people live, in a more technological, digital age where all our actions, our employment, our purchases, are monitored and assessed for their carbon neutrality. Well, if that is what is needed to save the planet, you may think. This is what some people call the 'Fourth Industrial Revolution' or the 'Great Reset'. Ironically, in consensus and cooperation with the government, XR don't want to talk about that. Why? If these changes were better for society and the environment, you would be shouting plans for the future from the rooftops. But corporations and governements aren't restricted, and this mitigation comes at the price of a lot more control and stifling of our freedoms. This could include restrictions in protest while that social change is forced through. The fight here is no longer about environmentalism, it's about creating a situation to bring about social change. This is clearly why so many social justice movements have been hijacked by light/bright green environmentalists who want to make people change the way they do things, but not corporations as long as they offset their carbon output or plant a few trees.

To anyone not giving it much thought, it seems like XR are raising awareness of what needs to change, but shutting down London for ten days wasn't going to save the environment. Physically stopping the industrialisation of our countryside, standing in the way of more road building, and protecting and creating green spaces in our communities would be much more beneficial to the planet and society. But where are XR protests at the HS2 (High Speed railway) sites, where vast acres of ancient woodland throughout the West Midlands are being destroyed for a slightly faster rail link from London to Birmingham? Surely thousands of people blocking a port for ten days, to highlight shipping's contribution to CO2, would carry more substance to the cause if it really was all about the environmental crisis. Actions such as disrupting plastic producing companies, would have had a bigger impact and been supported by *all* environmentalists. However, they'd rather shut down parts of London than actually stand in the way of genuine environmental devastation. With thousands of XR protesters having no idea of the history of their leaders' involvement in protest denial, they unknowingly started to provide the evidence the government needed to build a case for restricting protest.

I had never witnessed the volume of mainstream media coverage that Extinction Rebellion received: grassroots protests in comparison get limited media coverage. Moreover, apart from a few rumblings from the political establishment, XR were largely free to do as they pleased for ten days. No other protest group, outside the middle-classes, would have been allowed to shut London down as they did, and certainly not for that length of time. A boat was even able to be brought in at one location, blocking a busy area of London for many days. Was the significance of the boat in Oxford circus not infact about climate change, but changing the law on objects on highways, including short term lock-ons? Regardless, the more disruption there was, the better for the government, because it gets the general public's back up, who then demand tougher measures to deal with protests, without thought about what it means for their personal freedoms in the future. Any movement needs support, but XR tactics seemed targeted at losing support. All my previous experience in protest had shown me that the authorities and the local and national media had used the discourse of disruption to life in the community, blocking of blue light routes and so on, when influencing public opinion.

Anyone who protects the environment has my full support, but the aims of XR leaders, when you look closely, do not deal directly with the environmental crisis. They are more about mitigation polices, which tend to restrict poorer communities' ways of doing things, while the middle and upper classes, and businesses, carry on as they were apart from a bit of carbon offsetting. So, we're all being told to change our petrol cars to electric ones by 2030, yet CEOs of companies will continue to fly in private jets, producing a lot more carbon emissions, to hour-long meetings on the other side of the world. When you start mitigating for climate change, anything can be bartered in return for help, including rights to protest against real dangers and threats to our lives. No doubt, some of them feel it is a price worth paying, but for poorer communities, protest is a lifeline. Adaption policies are the way forward, from what I can see, to help communities adapt to the effects of climate change. For example, in Bangladesh, where the sea level is rising rapidly and coastline houses are at great risk of being flooded, houses are being built on stilts and fish farms created to give people a living. Adapting to what is happening to our planet is something humans and animals have always done. However, this often involves migration, which isn't something our government promotes.

In total, some 1200 people were arrested throughout the ten days. Of course, grassroots XR supporters, regular people who want to save the environment for further degradation, are not to blame because they believe they are doing something vitally important. I suspect ninety nine percent of those 'rebels' in XR had no idea they could be working to create a totalitarian protest law, as they are too brainwashed by the fear generated by professional climate change agents to see the bigger picture.

Cressida Dick, the Metropolitan Police Commissioner, asked for help because of XR's actions. Weeks later, she began raising the question of tougher laws, to deter similar demonstrations. In an article by the Evening Standard, she was quoted as saying, "Although they caused major disruption, the offences committed were not serious and therefore the deterrent is not significant."

Getting arrested with the PNR4 after our grassroots direct action against Cuadrilla

Celebrating outside Manchester Civil Courts after railroading the protest pen

Community members leading the resistance against Marriott Drilling Company

The Frack Free community resistance of Frack Free Ryedale

Celebrating everyone's acquittal of unlawful Marriott arrests

The local community resistance upsets Tina Rothery

Tower but no resistance from the proclaimed leaders

Masters graduation day with two of my lecturers

Ready for my first appearance at the Court of Appeal

Celebrating the victory with grassroots campaigners in Lancashire

The Liverpool Echo Environment Awards 2019

Twenty-Six

Frackers Come to my Town – and I Object on A Whole New Level

THE SUMMER OF 2019 began with me recieving the Healthy Living award at the Echo Environment Awards 2019. The awards ceremony, in association with executive sponsors Merseyrail, were hosted by BBC's Roger Johnson who paid tribute to the late TV presenter and friend, Dianne Oxberry. In its eigth year, the awards ceremony held at the Gladstone theatre in Sefton, recognises the outstanding work businesses and the community go through to protect the environment. My MSc dissertation, measuring air pollution indoors and outdoors at primary schools, in connection with the Green Schools Project won us the award. I was elated. It was a fantastic night and an honour to be a part of the evening.

Late summer, a planning application to drill and frack at Great Altcar, near Formby, just five miles from my home, was at the consultation stage. Although Formby is in the borough of Sefton, Merseyside, the planning application hearing for Altcar would occur at Lancashire County Council, which was not favourable, what with all the agents the industry had already accumulated in this area over the previous five years. Maureen Mills lived in Halsall, just a few miles from the proposed drill site, which positioned her at the heart of the local campaign, again centralising the information/data with the FFL hierarchy. Remember, her husband was a manager of an offshore oil and gas company, and she was a councillor.

I attended a public meeting in Formby with a good friend George Nicholas, who also lived a few miles from the proposed site. I was disappointed to hear the whole focus of the event was on climate change, not the wanton destruction of land, air and water due to fracking. By now, we had already long established that fracked gas would be a by-product for producing plastics, and raising this issue nationally had proved to be the most successful community approach with which to oppose the industry. When it came to the Q&A, I was quick to my feet to point this connection to the plastics industry, and the room was shocked by my revelation. I was shocked that they didn't know this. But the overall angle of this meeting further confirmed my beliefs; these people were using the application as a mind-changing exercise for the climate change social change agenda. Of course, I knew much more, but it would have been far too much for most in the room to comprehend, so I stayed quiet.

I decided from that day forward that I would keep my distance from that campaign and focus on my own approach. I had already created a local Frack Free group in Liverpool and Sefton, which would be beneficial later if the council passed the application. By now, the majority of local anti-fracking groups online, had been taken over by the climate change narrative. However, with my now in-depth knowledge of the campaign, the legal system and my two degrees, I decided to object to the plans personally. Previously, I had only objected to fracking proposals with my feet on the ground, and arms in lock-ons, but with all the information I had recently uncovered, I thought I'd rock their boat, where no one else was. By this point, I'd had enough of objection templates created by climate groups, directing me on how I should oppose applications.

This objection was the first time an application for exploration of hydrocarbons was objected to on different grounds, quite possibly anywhere in the world. Still, I believed it was of crucial importance for local and national democracy. You see, the application did not refer to the Nationally Significant Infrastructure Policy (NSIP) or the National Policy Statement (NPS) for Geological Disposal

Infrastructure 2019, which I believed it should. Furthermore, it did not refer to the requirement to use data from the proposed borehole to support the search for Geological Disposal Facilities (GDF) or deep geological borehole disposal for radioactive nuclear waste and other toxic wastes. Funnily enough, current planning policy meant that the initial permission for boreholes is the democratically accountable decision of the Planning Committees. Still, the local community may have no control over this or any subsequent development. Therefore, I suggested the application was incomplete.

The proposed exploratory boreholes were for oil and gas, but the geological data obtained would be reported regularly to the Department for Business, Energy and Industrial Strategy (BEIS) and the British Geological Survey (BGS). I believed this direct connection with the urgent need to find GDF sites meant the applicant should identify the NSIP process at the beginning of any exploratory borehole application. Aurora Energy, the company involved, made no mention of the broader use of data from exploratory drilling of the proposed borehole; therefore, I believed it incomplete. I suggested the council should not decide until the background facts detailed were presented for consideration by the Planning Committee after full public consultation and debate.

In consideration of previous similar applications at Preston New Road, Harthill and Marsh Lane, there was no reference by the applicant, community representatives or the Secretary of State at the BEIS to the national importance of the data for deep geological disposal as part of a GDF. In those applications, the government overturned the planning committee's decisions to reject the proposed exploratory boreholes by the planning inspectorate without reference to borehole data for NSIP research. Therefore, not only were fracking companies avoiding this issue, but the government were avoiding it too. Why? The government had already achieved data collection for broader use in research to identify geological disposal facilities for nuclear waste without any reference to a material consideration that is of immediate relevance to any local community.

In the previous years, one could go on the council's planning site and read objections from other community members, but now they had conveniently stopped that too. Why? I believe this was hiding specific complaints, so the broader community could not see them. The last thing the authorities wanted was people linking opposing applications together, nor would they like the wider public viewing my objection, which focused on the whole process, including geological disposal. I emailed the details of my objection to every councillor in Sefton and West Lancashire, and not one replied or asked a further question. *Representative democracy? Don't make me laugh*, I thought.

Thankfully, the application never got past this stage when, strangely, Aurora decided one day to remove the application altogether. With many important wildlife sites nearby, I would hope it would have been rejected anyway. I have no idea of my influence in the decision, but I do know the last thing the government wants is the general population learning about the link between fracking and geological disposal of nuclear waste. Throughout the INEOS injunction, this was one of my reasons for challenging, because the last thing I wanted was for trucks of radioactive waste coming through local communities, without any say or resistance in the matter. But now, with the XR agents/actors continuing their drive to support the new Home Office Minister Priti Patel, I remained suspicious that the government wanted to shut down protest before they moved into the next phase of draconian measures, one being implementing nuclear toxic waste disposal on vulnerable communities. I might have been wrong in my assumptions, but still, I was following my conscience.

A new atomic sector is impossible in the UK without first finding somewhere to isolate the vast amount of waste stored at Sellafield in Cumbria. This issue is not a conspiracy, even though the climate change agents/actors label it just that. A government white paper on radioactive waste disposal makes it clear that they need somewhere to store it. Of course, they do, you can't have nuclear power without nuclear waste. With the building of a new nuclear power station at Hinckley Point, that stored waste needs to go somewhere first.

The government claims that its priority is a GDF underground that will hold all our waste, keeping it in one place. However, building this facility will take some thirty years, and the government has not yet even found a location or a welcoming community. Many people, including myself, believe this is a secondary reason for borehole drilling around the country in rural areas. It makes sense because in the US and Australia wells were drilled and fracked at a phenomenal pace, whereas in the UK, it was pedestrian. No more than a few dozen wells compared to thousands in the US and Australia, and except for a few, these wells have yet to be fracked, if ever.

The only people making money from fracking, at this point, were those in the know able to manipulate the stock market. Evidence shows that every time a positive statement was made by the oil and gas industry regarding fracking, the share price rose and soon declined. In effect, investors paid for the drilling of wells, so no cost to the companies themselves; those who knew when announcements would be made, would have made huge profits.

Representatives from the nuclear lobby, national government, and drilling companies (most notably P R Marriott Drilling Ltd) have been at many alleged fracking exploratory sites. Several universities, including Sheffield and Lancashire, have been working on deep geological disposal research for some years. In 2015, the year the Infrastructure Act was passed, the Director of P R Marriott Drilling Ltd John Deswick, alongside Professor Fergus Gibb and Dr Karl Travis, Department of Materials Science and Engineering, were awarded the George Stephenson Medal. This award was for their paper titled 'Deep Borehole Disposal of Nuclear Waste: Engineering Challenges'. That was over five years ago, and research has continued worldwide, which has led to a new disposal concept called 'deep isolation'. A technology tested at a commercial drilling facility in the US, where a prototype canister was lowered 2200 ft into an existing borehole using a wireline cable. The canister was forced over 400 ft. (122 meters) using an underground 'tractor' into a long horizontal storage section. Is it only a coincidence that directional horizontal drilling is a crucial feature of hydraulic fracturing technology?

In the US, informed consent is a minimum requirement for deep isolation. The industry attempts to partner a strong understanding with communities on the safety and benefits that could materialise from isolating the waste instead of waiting to find a GDF. But, of course, burying radioactive nuclear waste underground is neither safe or beneficial. Evidence shows that Radioactive Waste Management (RWM) are working on this 'informed consent' here in the UK, but only by engaging with a minority of community representatives, the *discourse of cooperation and consensus* in action again. There has been no wide-spread information campaign about nuclear waste GDFs at all – unsurprisingly given how vehemently communities opposed fracking.

This scant community liaison process or Public Stakeholder Engagement (PSE) is dangerously open for nuclear industry lobbyists within the neighbourhood to control the process. Again, it's another flaw in stakeholder participation or citizen assemblies on deciding our future as communities. If trucks with nuclear waste did roll through the English countryside to be stored underground in fields outside unsuspecting villages and towns, would XR be protesting against it? I doubt it, the agents would be orchestrating consensus and cooperation.

Twenty-Seven

The End of Fracking? And the End of Protest, Too?

SOME THIRTY MONTHS after the land preparation, Cuadrilla began fracking the second well, known as PNR2, in August 2019. By now, the controlled opposition had total control of the road, and on some days, there would not be one activist there. The psychological abuse of many good local campaigners, over a long period, had now taken its toll. However, after just eleven days, Cuadrilla suspended these fracking operations following the UK's most significant fracking-induced tremor measuring 2.9 on the Richter scale. There were 134 similar events reported by the British Geological Survey during the short process, which eventually led to the moratorium on fracking, which still stands today.

The anti-fracking community had been campaigning on precisely this earthquake issue for years because we had evidence from Oklahoma of seismic activity from fracking, and the effect that had on land and water for miles around. Not even an apology for our treatment from police forces or the government has followed. Many people have faced fines, loss of liberty, family breakdowns, and more importantly great damage to their health from the gaslighting treatment received from state actors and climate agents. This psychological damage remains with many for the rest of our lives, all for doing what was right and just. Have any of the people who spent nights in tents and protesting day after day been awarded damages for their arrests? The answer is no. Have those people who were arrested and charged despite highlighting the dangers been compensated? No. What it does highlight though, is the importance of grassroots community resistance and how essential it is for this to take place unrestricted.

Predictably, very cleverly, the majority of these grassroots online anti-fracking groups have now been largely taken over by XR agents/ actors promoting only the climate change message. They had done what they set out to do from the start: make it all about climate change, and restrict real protest, but they weren't finished yet.

More protests, more restrictions
In line with the XR agreed protest in the spring, their next big action in autumn 2019 was headquartered at Trafalgar Square. After eight days, the Met announced it was ending the only legitimate protest site at nine o' clock on the evening of Monday the fifteenth of October. Cressida Dick put a blanket S14 on the demonstration across the whole of London. This was later squashed under judicial review because it went beyond the powers granted by police in the Public Order Act 1986, and rightfully so. Clear evidence of how Dick would have used the INEOS injunction earlier that May, if she'd had that option. Nevertheless, it was another failed attempt by the XR, RTP and Occupy agents to do the work of Dick and Patel, by setting a case precedent on protest restriction within the judicial system over a city-wide area.

Thankfully, there are many good people in XR, who can't all be swayed by the decisions of a few Occupy and RTP agents, who stood up and challenged the ban. If successful, it would have given the Home Office an escape route from a change in Public Order law. Would these people have stood up and challenged the protest ban if it was grassroots though? No chance: they had already proved that in INEOS case. They don't support grassroots, because it radically challenges the environmental crisis and because it puts power back into the people's hands. For these people, tackling climate change requires taking more power from the people.

During the eight days of demonstrations, the Met made 1828 arrests, but only ten percent of those arrests faced charges. Soon after, Dick confirmed that the police and government started discussions to change public order laws, including ways to hinder repeat offenders and 'disruption' - most notably, potential new offences relating to fixing things to the highway. Although, at first glance this would suggest objects like XR boats, it also means lock-on devices, vehicles, tractors, and so on, in grassroots protests.

A Home Office spokesperson said they were, "working with National Police Chiefs Council and the Metropolitan Police to look at how we could strengthen the police's powers to help manage unlawful protests." This organisation is the same NPCC that, alongside the CTPNOC, had advised INEOS to obtain injunctions against anti-frackers in 2017, setting the foundations for banning any protest not negotiated. The key framing in that sentence is 'unlawful', which specifically applies to static protests, not managed protests, so does not concern large climate change protests, which are all agreed. Furthermore, the government needs the climate change protests for legitimacy in social policy change as Bradbrook had confirmed earlier.

The involvement of the XR, Occupy and RTP agents participation with the Met, and no doubt other agencies, in planning the eradication of our protest rights, came from Cressida Dick herself. Dick wrote to Patel in December 2019, saying that the XR protests, "provided a much-needed opportunity for powers to curb protest." So, there it is, in black and white, a 'much-needed opportunity' was wanted because they had failed every step of the way through the judicial system, in earnest, since 2016. On top of that, in a letter released to the organisation Open Democracy, Dick told Patel that British laws should be changed to make it easier for police to ban protest. Ban protest that has not been agreed?

Opposition MPs and lawyers warned that changes to the law governing protest would damage democracy. Green Party MP Caroline Lucas, who supported my challenge in the INEOS case and whom I had always respected, until she allowed Rothery a Green

Party promotion, said Open Democracy's findings were, 'deeply worrying'. I would say having someone on your political party's national campaigns committee involved in the eradication of protest rights is also deeply worrying, but maybe she is unaware of Rothery's true colours. She soon won't be!

In September 2020, XR targeted newspaper printers in Broxbourne, Hertfordshire and Knowsley, near Liverpool, which blocked the day's newspapers. Was this blockade to provide the evidence for protecting supply chain protests? A government source, highlighted in the Canary, used the opportunity to claim the disruption had the potential, "for police to be handed beefed-up powers to stop protestors entering designated areas outside such premises." Not only do beefed up powers protect news printers, the powers protect all unethical businesses.

Six months later the UK lockdowns began for COVID 19 (Certification of Vaccine Identification), giving plenty of time and opportunity for the government to write new laws, whilst protest was restricted.

Twenty-Eight

The Draconian and Chilling Acts of Parliament

ON MARCH THE fifteenth 2021, the Home Office Minister Priti Patel brought forward the Police, Crime, Sentencing and Courts Bill 2021 (PCSC Bill). As I had predicted almost two years earlier, many of our successes at the Court of Appeal, were brought before the House of Commons. The Bill would allow the police to restrict or ban protest if it causes "serious annoyance" to the surrounding community, organisations and businesses, without a "reasonable excuse" punishable with a fine or up to ten years in prison. Grassroots unmanaged protest could have start and finish times on demonstrations, in line with managed protest. Failure to stick to managed protest conditions means people will face fines up to £2500. Basically, the bill hands over the power of deciding whether a protest is justified or should be allowed, primarily to the police.

I suspected the evidence for bringing in more draconian protest laws would be provided by Extinction Rebellion and RTP before them, and the detail of the bill clearly shows that. Importantly, where the Court of Appeal decided against implementing restrictive measures before the event, this bill does exactly that, so the public is criminalised without any evidence of criminal activity. It's a clear distinction between managed and unmanaged protests. During the

XR protests there were separate locations. But in the future, this would not be allowed to happen, only the centralised and designated area would be permitted. Was this why XR had different unmanaged protest locations?

It is essential not to get attached to the discourse linking the Black Lives Matter (BLM) protests to this bill. As already explained, this plan by the Met, Intelligence Services, climate change agents and the Home Office was in fruition long before the BLM protests, which in fact, came some six months after discussions of 'much-needed powers' between Dick and Patel. However, I believe the linking of the bill with BLM is purposeful, taking away blame from the white middle-class Occupy, RTP and XR leaders. Hardly surprising, with this racist government of Windrush generation deportations and shameful asylum-seeker accommodation scandals.

Another really dangerous Act was given Royal Assent just weeks earlier called the Covert Human Intelligence Services Act (CHIS Act 2021). Now, most of the talk is about the PCSC, (no surprise given that's what all the Kill the Bill protests are about) but the details of the CHIS Act 2021 are far more chilling. Basically, the security services can breach human rights, with no recourse. It means over 1200 undercover police officers, among many other organisations, including the Home Office, are protected if they break the law, lawfully, so their provocation could, legally, escalate, physically harming or even killing. The CHIS Act is deliberately vague about what crimes are to be permitted, stating that criminal conduct is necessary if it is, "in the interests of national security; for the purpose of preventing or detecting crime or of preventing disorder; or in the interests of the economic well-being of the United Kingdom."

This is dangerous with particular regard to protest groups because any effective grassroots movement, which the anti-fracking movement was, can experience undercover officers coming into a group as an agent provocateur, to deliberately stir up trouble and give the media ammunition to demonise the movement. Of course, this already happens but the Act will make it more widespread and lawful.

How many years has the mainstream media told us how bad certain countries are on human rights? Now, here we are on a similar, chilling path to the complete loss of human rights – and nobody's talking about it. The British Press didn't even report the CHIS Act until at least ten days after the Act was given Royal Assent.

It's worth noting that in 2017, Mark Roberts, Silver Commander at Barton Moss (2013-14), the North West Regional Lead on Public Order Policing, became NPCC Leader on Covert Legislation and Guidance. He would have had direct involvement in this new legislation. Was his guidance for this legislation to protect those very change agents/undercovers who had been working with him throughout the anti-fracking campaign in Northern England? If so, the question remains in law, are we still able to bring those involved historically to justice? The Labour Party, led by Sir Keir Starmer, whipped MPs to abstain from voting against the CHIS Act. Given Starmer's former role as Director of Public Prosecutions and Head of the Crown Prosecution Service, his decision is hardly surprising. But he was a human rights lawyer before that. Couldn't he see the dangers inherent in the CHIS bill?

Dan Carden, the Labour MP for Walton did, he resigned from the Labour front bench over the opposition government's decision, in doing so, received huge respect from the people of Liverpool. In his resignation, he said, "I share the deep concerns about this legislation from across the Labour movement, human rights organisations, and so many who have suffered the abuse of state power, from blacklisted workers to the Hillsborough families and survivors."

With a heavy heart, I feel the same.

The CHIS Bill dates back to a previously secret national security policy presented to Parliament in March 2018 (the Third Direction case), which ruled that undercover agents and informants could break the law in certain occasions. Unbelievably, that decision was made with a three to two majority of judges, prompting the government to rush the bill through without a legal challenge.

We are now seeing early signs of the use of the CHIS Act. On the twenty-fourth of April 2021 during Kill the Bill protests in Manchester, mostly attended by young people, a Green and Black Cross (GBC) legal observer reported on social media (before then removing content) that a police sargeant had confirmed that armed officers were given authority to use armed force for the protection of property. The CHIS Act talks about 'preventing disorder', before any criminal activity has taken place. So although the facts on this incident are unclear, it is a worrying development that could happen more and more. In contrast, earlier that week, XR activists smashed windows with hammers at HSBC HQ in Canary Wharf, London, and were given mainstream coverage with no threats from the Met about using armed force. If the GBC post is true, does this mean in the future, your life is at risk for damaging property unless you're a climate activist?

This brings me back to the PCSC Bill, which the Labour Party was also intending on abstaining on. Although the mainstream road to the Kill the Bill protests began at the Clapham Common Sarah Everard vigil, the fight began long ago, as I experienced, without any support from NGOs. After the death of Sarah Everard and the public outcry, the Labour party made a u-turn and voted against the bill. However, the bill still succeeded in a House of Commons vote, so is, at the time of writing, with the Parliamentary Committee. What was notable in the days leading up to the bill's discussion in Parliament, before the fatal Everard event, was that publicly only NETPOL was vociferous against it, promoting a Charter of Rights. Strangely, as soon as the Labour Party changed course, every mainstream NGO and petition organisation came out the woodwork.

Minimal changes happen without protest: look at the figures from petitions over the years, and you will find only a very few achieve anything. So, all these organisations promoting petitions against the bill may raise awareness, but not do much else. Furthermore, the managed demonstrations they promote are on the same footing, they just further government agenda without changing or stopping anything. Unless parts three and four of the Bill are stopped, the only people who will be lawfully allowed to protest will be NGOs and organisations the government is able to control, or the ones led by their change agents/actors – the 'controlled opposition'.

I have learned from the last eight years that any attempt to centralise a movement of people is an attempt to be state-managed, therefore no change will come. Grassroots won't be able to challenge anything in the future if the PCSC Bill becomes law. From now on, with police and intelligence services leading all movements covertly, with undercovers and other change agents taking lead roles, the chance of success of movements will depend on which ones the government want to further their cause.

We must watch very closely what the government does next in this oxymoron they call representative democracy. They may concede to XR demands to allow a stakeholder participation or citizen's assembly process. But then, the same people who have been working to eradicate protest are positioned as leaders and spokespersons, and likely to agree to new managed protest regulations and new draconian policies. A recent example of the people involved and the draconian policies these people have in mind was shown on the television show Good Morning Britain, in the last week in April 2021. A known lead change agent with Ocuupy and XR, Donnachadh McCarthy, declared people were selfish because they had pets because of their effect on climate change. People should be very worried about this statement because, for almost twenty years, these people have been changing minds and policies day by day. So it's not too far-fetched to expect these change agents plan the eradication of pets in the near future.

These climate change agents/actors and organisations involved in the attempted discursive eradication of our protest rights should be brought to justice, as they have collectively put our country and its people in great danger. They want to help implement draconian policies whilst denying us the right to oppose. It makes me wonder if those climate leaders who promote social change policies, not environmentalism, also support full-scale lockdowns and the loss of personal freedom. The evidence is clear to me that getting behind climate change organisations, such as XR, at this crucial time will lead us into an authoritarian state.

Perhaps there are some members of the population who believe people like me need restricting, I was, after all, arrested eight times. But I have only broken the law twice protesting and both times I was denied my right to protest, which I reacted to peacefully. Did I even break the law though? I was proven right in my actions to defend the environment. Nothing I did was criminal; the criminality lies on the industry's side and the government. Next time, that person being arrested could be you for protecting your community.

Fighting fracking, all communities outside of Lancashire were very successful because they welcomed other people's help and used a non-hierarchical approach to protests, all of which were non-violent. They may have been confrontational at times, of course, but that is inevitable when governments overrule local democracy and the police get heavy-handed. Some of this grassroots resistance was disruptive, but only short-term and always community-led. Only real social and environmental grassroots resistance with no hierarchy will bring any light at the end of this dark, dangerous tunnel we now face. Of course, I only have an environmental movement perspective with my view of XR, RTP and Occupy; no doubt these discursive change agents are in other campaigns, especially ones that are about social justice.

I highlighted the issue of radioactive waste disposal as just one possibility that could unfold. If nuclear fusion plants are to sprout up across the country, there will be a need to target communities with minimal resistance. People must be allowed, through local democracy, to decide their futures and be free to protest in doing so. No protest means communities restricted to their garden, under current trajectories, whilst the toxic trucks come sailing through guarded by police vehicles. You will then see how many of these XR rebels really care about the environment. And you will see how violent and oppressive the police and state can be.

Hopefully, by now, I have shown the dangers of giving the police more powers over protest. From my experience, they have more than enough powers already, which restrict protest. Grassroots campaigners will be imprisoned on remand for demonstrating lawfully, whilst waiting to be acquitted under new proposals. No community is safe from an authoritarian government and its leaders, just as the Conservative strongholds of North Yorkshire, East Yorkshire, West Sussex and Lancashire have found out in the past decade. It is not an attack on classes, this is an attack on everyone, by the corporate lobby, climate agents and the state.

However, as someone who lost his liberty, was assaulted and gaslighted by climate change agents/actors for radically protecting the environment and rights to protest, the last thing I want people to take away from this is a loss of where to go next. Personal sovereignty will be vital in protecting the environment and our freedoms, as governments and climate change agents are only interested in controlling every part of our lives. Walking down the road with a flag or a banner with a quasi-campaign name and symbol does more harm than good when it leads you away from personal sovereignity at a time when we all need to protect it.

The one thing I learned throughout this last decade was that people do care about their local environment and are instinctively willing to protect it without having to be told to by an umbrella NGO or protest group. It was interesting that when fracking stopped, due to the moratorium, anti-fracking group pages on social media became almost dormant, even with the attempted discourse of the climate change agent's takeover. Climate change posts in these groups got far fewer likes than any of our anti-fracking campaigning did. The decentralised anti-fracking movement captivated and inspired many people, like myself, who had never campaigned before, taking personal responsibility for their local area and standing up for what they know to be true and worth fighting for. We must allow this to continue and not have our lives dictated and restricted by governments or climate agents. This bravery is exactly what those now passed, who I met along the way did, including Thomas Burke, Deb Kay and her husband, Michelle Martin and others.

The growing Freedom Movement is leading the way on killing the bill, because fighting for personal freedom and protest rights go hand-in-hand, so my energies will support that path. Furthermore, the highest law lords in our country have already decided against such draconian measures before, in my case against INEOS. We have to trust they will use their wisdom and power to stop this out-of-control, oppressive juggernaut in its tracks and bring Britain back from the brink of authoritarianism. Failing that, in the words of John F Kennedy, "those who make peaceful revolution impossible, will make violent revolution inevitable", and that is not in the best interests of anyone.

We shouldn't expect any help from the BBC, their track record is abysmal for being on the side of the people. There are many online media sources to get an alternative view in these dangerous times, so no need for a one dimensional mainstream media angle. Therefore, it's now up to you, the people, to finish the job off and kill the bill, but time is running out.

Sadly, my friend and prolific campaigner Ian R Crane also passed away while I was writing this book, in February 2021, after a battle with cancer. His influence and direction were instrumental in our success in protecting the environment in communities right across northern England. His work on the Cuadrilla injunction, and those before, was the catalyst for my INEOS success. Therefore, he also leaves a legacy of protecting protest rights here in the UK and across the globe. He will be deeply missed by all who were graced by his intelligence and presence, and I hope my work here carries on his legacy.

If my turn comes next, you will know exactly why. I also hope I leave an inspiring and honourable legacy, and that, one day, everyone really will have a say in what happens in their community and we won't have to fight for our freedoms anymore.

BIBLIOGRAPHY

How fracking caused earthquakes in the UK, New Scientist: https://www.newscientist.com/article/dn21120-how-fracking-caused-earthquakes-in-the-uk/

Fracking Balcombe: A Threatened community 2010-2013, Frack Off: https://frack-off.org.uk/fracking-balcombe-a-threatened-community-2010-2013/

Top lawyer raises concern about number of arrests at Balcombe fracking protests, The Argus: https://www.theargus.co.uk/news/11220248.top-lawyer-raises-concerns-about-number-of-arrests-at-balcombe-fracking-protests/

Green MP Caroline Lucas as anti-fracking protests reach fever pitch, The Independent: https://www.independent.co.uk/news/uk/home-news/green-mp-caroline-lucas-arrested-anti-fracking-protests-reach-fever-pitch-8774189.html

Final Report - Shale Gas Extraction, The Royal Society: https://royalsociety.org/topics-policy/projects/shale-gas-extraction/report/

Fracking protestors set up camp in Salford, BBC News: https://www.bbc.co.uk/news/uk-england-manchester-24983918

Gilmore, J, Jackson, WH and Monk, HL (2016) *Keep Moving! Report on the Policing of the Barton Moss Community Protection Camp, November 2013-April 2014*. Centre for the Study of Crime, Criminalisation & Social Exclusion, LJMU and Centre for URBan research, University of York, Liverpool: https://www.ljmu.ac.uk/~/media/files/ljmu/research/centres-and-institutes/ccse/bm_final_170216_email.pdf?la=en

GM Police accused of quotas: as five arrested in Barton Moss, Salford Star: https://www.salfordstar.com/article.asp?id=2067

New Cheshire Chief Constable Mark Roberts steps in to lead force, Nantwich News: https://thenantwichnews.co.uk/2021/04/27/new-cheshire-chief-constable-mark-roberts-steps-in-to-lead-force/

Anti-fracking protest camp in Barton Moss searched after flare fired at police helicopter, Manchester Evening News: https://www.manchestereveningnews.co.uk/news/greater-manchester-news/anti-fracking-protest-camp-barton-moss-6471673

Fracking: Cameron Offers Councils Drill Money, Sky News: https://news.sky.com/story/fracking-cameron-offers-councils-drill-money-10421695

David Cameron goes 'all out for shale' with tax boost for councils willing to approve projects, The Independent: https://www.independent.co.uk/news/uk/politics/david-cameron-promises-fracking-tax-boost-councils-willing-approve-projects-9055280.html

Greater Manchester Police: Barton Moss arrests case set to collapse, Salford Star: https://www.salfordstar.com/article.asp?id=2144

Barton Moss: Rise of the Resistance, The Greenman. https://thesnufkin.blogspot.com/2014/05/barton-moss-rise-of-resistance.html

Chester Anti Fracking protests 'premature', BBC News: https://www.bbc.co.uk/news/uk-england-manchester-26931594

City of London versus Samede, High Court: https://www.judiciary.uk/wp-content/uploads/JCO/Documents/Judgments/cityoflondon-v-samede.pdf

Fracking protestors set up camp near possible test site, ITV News: https://www.itv.com/news/calendar/story/2014-05-12/fracking-protestors-set-up-camp-near-possible-test-site/

Fracking Application rejected by Lancashire county council, The Guardian: https://www.theguardian.com/environment/2015/jun/29/fracking-application-cuadrilla-rejected-lancashire-county-council

What is a Structural Adjustment Program? Smart Capital Mind: https://www.smartcapitalmind.com/what-is-a-structural-adjustment-program.htm

What is the Kyoto Protocaol, UNFCC: https://unfccc.int/kyoto_protocol

Climate Camp disbanded, The Guardian: https://www.theguardian.com/environment/2011/mar/02/climate-camp-disbanded

Anti-fracking protest camp set up near Tarleton, Lancashire, BBC News: https://www.bbc.co.uk/news/uk-england-lancashire-22477559

Fracking: Benefits, council house and non stop partying, Tough old life being protestor!, Daily Mail Online: https://www.dailymail.co.uk/news/article-2401253/Fracking-Benefits-council-house-non-stop-partying-Tough-old-life-protester.html

Gas company seeks to bankrupt anti-fracking campaigner, Drill or Drop: https://drillordrop.com/2015/12/23/gas-company-seeks-to-bankrupt-anti-fracking-campaigner/

Campaigners declare victory as Rathlin abandons Crawberry Hill over costs, Drill or Drop: https://drillordrop.com/2015/08/13/campaigners-declare-victory-as-rathlin-abandons-crawberry-hill-over-costs/

West newton Earth Warriors Released, Occupy London: https://occupylondon.org.uk/west-newton-earth-warriors-released/

Undercover, The True Story of Britain's Secret Police, Respubca: https://respubca.home.xs4all.nl/pdf/21undercoverthetruestoryofbritainssecretpolice.pdf

Arrests Made At Crawberry Hill, VIKING FM: https://planetradio.co.uk/viking/local/news/arrests-made-crawberry-hill/

INEOS adds to shale gas licence holdings, Drill or Drop: https://drillordrop.com/2017/03/09/ineos-adds-to-shale-gas-licence-holdings/?share=google-plus-1

Shale Gas and Plastic Industries Converge, Thermoo Fisher Scientific: https://www.thermofisher.com/blog/materials/shale-gas-and-plastic-industries-converge/

'*Reclaim the Power*' *anti-fracking camp*, Reclaim the Power: https://earthworker2013.wordpress.
com/2014/08/27/reclaim-the-power-anti-fracking-action-camp/

Arrest Made at Crawberry Hill, Viking FM: https://planetradio.co.uk/viking/local/news/
arrests-made-crawberry-hill/

General Election: Green Party candidate Tina Rothery, Alderleyedge.com: https://www.
alderleyedge.com/news/article/11446/general-election-green-party-candidate-tina-rothery

Vivienne Westwood drives tank to David Cameron house in anti-fracking protest, The
Independent: https://www.independent.co.uk/news/people/vivienne-westwood-drives-tank-
david-cameron-s-house-anti-fracking-protest-10496728.html

Fracking Given Green Light in North Yorkshire, Sky News: https://news.sky.com/story/
fracking-given-green-light-in-north-yorkshire-10292389

*Lancashire Fracking Deision: Sajid Javid Overules Council to say controversial drilling will take
place at Preston New Road*, HuffPost UK: https://www.huffingtonpost.co.uk/entry/lancashire-
fracking-decision_uk_57f605cfe4b012652682080e

Vivienne Westwood returns to Upton Protection Camp as eviction threat looms, Cheshire Live:
https://www.cheshire-live.co.uk/news/chester-cheshire-news/vivienne-westwood-returns-
upton-protection-10554323

Upton anti-fracking camp: Arrests made at eviction, BBC News: https://www.bbc.co.uk/news/
uk-england-merseyside-35292124

North Yorkshire fracking vote Council approves fracking in Ryedale, The Independent: https://
www.independent.co.uk/news/uk/home-news/north-yorkshire-fracking-vote-council-
approves-fracking-ryedale-a7044086.html

Cuadrilla boss ueged to drop case against Lancashire fracking 'nana', Campaign against Climate
Change: http://www.campaigncc.org/iamtinatoo

Anti-fracking activist Tina Rothery spared £55k legal bill, BBC News: https://www.bbc.co.uk/
news/uk-england-lancashire-38267928

£21k left on doorstep 'as donation to Lytham St Anne's development, Daily Mail Online:
https://www.dailymail.co.uk/news/article-2102290/21k-left-doorstep-donation-Lytham-St-
Annes-development.html

The impact of Fracking on local residents in Blackpool and the Fylde Coast, Great British Life:
*https://www.greatbritishlife.co.uk/people/the-impact-of-fracking-on-local-residents-in-blackpool-
and-6933248*

Confirmed Oklahoma Earthquakes Caused by Fracking, EcoWatch: https://www.ecowatch.
com/confirmed-oklahoma-earthquakes-caused-by-fracking-1882034344.html

Earthquake of 4.6 magnitude in British Columbia caused by fracking says regulator, The
Independent: https://www.independent.co.uk/news/world/americas/earthquake-of-4-6-
magnitude-in-british-columbia-caused-by-fracking-says-regulator-a6781261.html

Updated: Campaigners occupy rig at Third Energy's Kirby Misperton Fracking site, Drill or Drop: https://drillordrop.com/2017/10/21/campaigners-occupy-rig-at-third-energys-kirby-misperton-fracking-site/

Campaigner to fight Ineos in court over order curbing fracking protests, The Guardian: https://www.theguardian.com/environment/2017/sep/11/campaigner-challenges-ineos-in-court-over-order-curbing-fracking-protests

What the judge said in his ruling on INEOS fracking protest injunction, Drill or Drop: https://drillordrop.com/2017/11/23/what-the-judge-said-in-his-ruling-on-ineos-fracking-protest-injunction/

Talking to the Cops, NETPOL: https://netpol.org/2019/03/13/talking-to-the-cops/

When is it in the Public Interest for the CPS to drop your case, Stoke Newington Chambers: https://stokenewingtonchambers.co.uk/when-is-it-in-the-public-interest-for-the-cps-to-drop-your-case/

High Court upholds "draconian" injunction granted to fracking company INEOS, Leigh Day: https://www.leighday.co.uk/latest-updates/news/2017-news/high-court-upholds-draconian-injunction-granted-to-fracking-company-ineos/

Meet the Yorkshire villages fighting the Frackers, The Guardian: https://drillordrop.com/2018/06/01/judge-grants-temporary-injunction-against-protests-at-lancashire-fracking-site/

Court of Appeal to hear fracking injunction "test case". Leigh Day: https://www.leighday.co.uk/latest-updates/news/2019-news/court-of-appeal-to-hear-fracking-injunction-test-case/

"Caravan of Love" fracking trial dropped "in public interest", Drill or Drop: https://drillordrop.com/2020/06/18/caravan-of-love-fracking-trial-dropped-in-public-interest/

5 Badass Women Protecting the Planet this International Women's Day: Greenpeace: https://medium.com/greenpeace/5-badass-women-protecting-the-planet-this-international-womens-day-2f844d65b88f

Anti-fracking campaigners win appeal on the right to protest, Leigh Day: https://www.leighday.co.uk/latest-updates/news/2019-news/anti-fracking-campaigners-win-appeal-on-the-right-to-protest/

Extinction Rebellion protest activity at Marble Arch 20 April, Marble Arch London: https://marble-arch.london/news/extinction-rebellion-at-marble-arch/

From Monday 15 April: Extinction Rebellion to block Marble Arch, Oxford Circus, Waterloo Bridge & Parliament Sq round the clock until Government acts on Climate Emergency, Extinction Rebellion: https://extinctionrebellion.uk/2019/04/09/from-monday-15-april-extinction-rebellion-to-block-marble-arch-oxford-circus-waterloo-bridge-parliament-sq-round-the-clock-until-government-acts-on-climate-emergency%EF%BB%BF/

Met chief Cressida Dick: 'Extinction Rebellion protestors caught us out', London Evening Standard: https://www.standard.co.uk/news/crime/met-chief-cressida-dick-extinction-rebellion-protesters-in-london-caught-us-out-a4142231.html

Ministers meeting with eco rabble plotting to bring London to a halt tommorrow, Daily Mail Online: https://www.dailymail.co.uk/news/article-6919593/Ministers-meeting-eco-rabble-plotting-bring-London-halt-tomorrow.html

Ministers looking into clampdown on XR and beefed-up police powers after press blockade protest, The Canary: https://www.thecanary.co/uk/news/2020/09/06/ministers-looking-into-clampdown-on-xr-and-beefed-up-police-powers-after-press-blockade-protest/

The Government is legalising and extending the infamous spycop's criminal actions and you could be a victim, The Canary: https://www.thecanary.co/feature/2020/10/12/the-government-is-legalising-and-extending-this-infamous-spycops-criminal-action/

Nick Ferrari Challenges Met Commissioner Cressida Dick Over Extinction Rebellion Pink Yacht, LBC: https://www.lbc.co.uk/radio/presenters/nick-ferrari/met-commissioner-extinction-rebellion-pink-yacht/

Dan Carden Resigns from Labour Frontbench over CHIS Bill, Tribune: https://www.tribunemag.co.uk/2020/10/exclusive-dan-carden-resigns-from-labour-frontbench-over-chis-bill

Met Police Chief urged Priti Patel to use Extinction Rebellion 'opportunity' to curb protest rights, Open Democracy: https://www.opendemocracy.net/en/met-police-chief-urged-priti-patel-to-use-extinction-rebellion/

Police, Crime, Sentencing and Courts Bill publication: Parliamentary Bills, UK Parliament: https://bills.parliament.uk/bills/2839/publications

Covert Human Intelligence Sources (Criminal Conduct) Act 2021-Parliamentary Bills, UK Parliament: https://bills.parliament.uk/bills/2783

UK set to pass bill allowing police, gov't agents to break laws when 'necessary', Life Site News. https://www.lifesitenews.com/news/uk-set-to-pass-bill-allowing-police-govt-agents-to-break-law-when-necessary

Crime Bill makes fracking protests impossible, Yorkshire Post: https://www.yorkshirepost.co.uk/news/opinion/letters/crime-bill-makes-fracking-protests-impossible-yorkshire-post-letters-3192236

Printed in Great Britain
by Amazon

79483993R10129